A Thousand Little Memories

A Mother's Brave Pilgrimage To Reclaim JOY after Traumatic Loss

Julie Green

A Thousand Little Memories
Julie Green

Published by
HOPE Publishing House
4756 Crawford Gulch Road
Golden, CO 80403
www.HopePublishingHouse.com
Lisa@LisaJCoaching.com
954.829.5693

ISBN: 979-8-9917952-1-0 (Hardcover)
ISBN: 979-8-9917952-0-3 (eBook)

Manufactured in the United States
10 9 8 7 6 5 4 3 2

Editors: Auriana Renee and Vicki McCown
Book Layout: Opeyemi Ikuborije
Cover Art: Lorne Cramer, lornecramer@gmail.com

Praise for
A Thousand Little Memories

"Julie Green's courageously gritty approach to grief glows with strength, grace, and deep faith. I can attest to the fact that Julie is an amazing trail buddy, and though this is not a trail I would have ever wished for her, I am grateful that she has chosen to walk us through her healing journey, so that we also may reclaim joy."

Tracy L. Maxwell

"Through the courageous and deeply personal story of her own unimaginable loss, Julie Green walks us through the raw, difficult journey of grieving her son's suicide. Her honesty, vulnerability, and wisdom offer comfort to those of us navigating pain, showing that while grief may never fully leave us, healing and hope are possible. This book is a powerful guide for anyone who feels lost in their sorrow, providing a path to finding peace on the other side."

Lisa Ponsford, Nurse Practitioner and Associate Professor

"In this book, Julie Green travels a road of immeasurable loss, but the journey has somehow given her a strength she may have never known otherwise. Every step has led her closer to her true purpose."

Leanne Link

"Anyone who is on a similar journey of healing will benefit from this testimony of hope and courage. Julie Green's writing has already helped me to look towards the light of my dark and painful memories and begin to share that light."

Beverly Knox

"This book is a deeply moving experience. Julie's raw and beautiful account of losing her son to suicide will touch every reader deeply. Her strength in sharing this journey and finding light amidst darkness is truly inspirational. Through her insightful prose, she reminds us all that love can transform pain, helping us to see beauty in everyday moments and find hope even in the hardest times."

Denise Gosselin Stanek

"*A Thousand Little Memories* provides a usable blueprint of transformation for anyone who has experienced loss. Julie passionately weaves together the realities of the pain with elements of the scientific, the pragmatic, and the spiritual to lead the reader through acceptance and growth."

Trish Feaster Cook, Tour Guide and Travel Writer, *The Travelphile*

"It is amazing that from great darkness came such a beautiful light. Your heart will break with Julie's, but you will peek glimmers of hope and gain comfort as you navigate through grief. A must-read for anyone experiencing the loss of a loved one."

Georgeana Ireland, Artist, Ethos Contemporary Art

"Julie's story will inspire readers to embark on their own journey toward a better life, regardless of their past experiences. Her practical healing strategies are invaluable for anyone who has faced loss of any kind."

Sandi Derby, GRM Advanced Certified Grief Recovery Specialist

"I am so inspired by Julie's grit and determination to take unimaginable tragedy and create a life so amazing not only for herself but for others."

Robyne Wood, Founder, Robyne's Nest

"Julie journeys up the Mountains of Grief with integrity, faith, curiosity, and love. This engaging book will help so many. And to my soul sister… I thank you for giving this to the universe. You are a true gift."

Renie Muratore

"*A Thousand Little Memories* is a must-read for those who are dealing with tragic loss, especially that of a child. The book provides hope for moving forward from the deepest sadness and finding new meaning and joy in life."

Jennifer Smith

"Heart-wrenching yet uplifting, *A Thousand Little Memories* offers a comforting embrace for anyone who has experienced loss. Don't miss the cover—a thousand little photographic memories of Jack—a truly beautiful testament to a mother's enduring love."

Kelly Lorene Cummings, Author of *It's a Lifestyle Thing*

"To anyone who has lost a child and thinks you will never recover, you need to hear Julie Green's story. Julie knows the excruciating pain and hopelessness, but through her journey she has achieved deep healing. She will provide you with much-needed hope and the belief that you can get through this."

Anne-Marie Lockmyer, Grief Specialist, CCISD, CTIP, Grief & Trauma Healing Network, LLC

"Thank you to Julie Green for sharing her heart, her journey of healing, and, most importantly, Jack. Her story and the Grief Recovery Method's place in it truly touched my heart. Julie expertly weaves her own lessons learned with visions of the healing that's possible for the grieving people who read this book or work with her in the future."

Cole James, President, The Grief Recovery Institute

Acknowledgements

First, I want to thank God for being my guiding light through the darkness.

Thank you to Lisa Jimenez, my mindset coach, writing coach, mentor, and friend, for all the life-changing lessons. Her tireless support through the process of writing this book has been incredible, and I feel extremely blessed to have met her.

To Auriana Renee I give much appreciation for her amazing skill as my writing coach and editor. She made my words sound so much better with a wave of her magic word-processing wand. I am so grateful for her understanding of language and unique talent for seeing that golden thread woven through all my stories.

To Vicki McCown, my "picky Vicki," who did a superb job of editing my final manuscript: I didn't even cry when I saw all that red! I am so grateful for her eagle eyes on every page of the book.

Thank you to Lorne Cramer for the beautiful book cover art. It is absolutely perfect!

To my parents Pat and Larry Mertens, thanks for having my back and believing in me through this entire process.

Thank you to my sons Joshua and James for their continued words of encouragement and support from afar.

To my daughter Tori, special thanks for putting up with me writing for hours on end at the kitchen table and for all the "coffee talk" breaks I needed.

Thank you to all of my family and friends who stood by me through this long process of missing events and forgoing time together in order to get this done. They are what make life worth living and I appreciate every one of them.

Thank you to Kim Webb, Laura Zabicki, and Betsy Blackburn, mothers united in loss of a son, who each honored me by sharing their story to be used in my book. I am forever grateful for their courage and vulnerability.

To my brother Jimmy, who I now realize has been with me all these years as a guardian angel, thank you. He was my first friend and, although he was only fifteen months older than me, took care of me then and now.

Finally, to my son Jack: thank you for being in my life for a brief but wonderful nineteen years. You changed who I am in this world. You will continue to be my travel companion in spirit for every adventure and milestone. I will carry you in my heart until the day I pass over and we are reunited.

Dedication

I dedicate this book to my children.

All four very different, and all valued equally.

You are the reason I am who I am,
and you all share a part of my heart.

To the readers of this book who have suffered
a loss, may you find peace and comfort in the
chapters and embark on your own pilgrimage to
reclaim joy once more.

CONTENTS

Foreword

*by The Reverend Canon
Cindy Evans Voorhees*

When I think of Julie Green, the word that comes to mind is resilience. In my twenty years as a priest, I have never encountered anyone quite like her. Julie has been a parishioner of mine for several years and witnessing her miraculous journey through the tragedy of losing her son, Jack, to such a gruesome suicide has been a privilege. Her strength, determination, self-awareness, kindness in the face of unbearable emotional pain, and deep love for her family and friends are not just inspiring—they are real.

I have been the priest called to give comfort to many grieving parents who have faced similar unimaginable news. How could this happen? Why didn't they see it coming? Their worst nightmare now a crippling reality. But Julie is one of the few parents I have seen who did not give up—on Jack or herself. She sought out answers, finding tools to cope and heal, not only for herself but for all of us.

Julie found refuge in the church by interring Jack in our chapel. This allowed her to be with him on Sunday mornings and visit our columbarium, leaving flowers and tokens of love near his niche. She meticulously reviewed the last few months of his life, leaving no stone unturned in her search for meaning in the senseless act of suicide. Julie educated herself on grief and recovery, attending classes, leaning into support groups, and confiding in those she trusted. She read, researched, and sometimes screamed into the wind at the beach—only to feel her son's presence, gripping her heart and telling her he was at peace with God.

My journey with Julie has, in turn, helped me guide others. I have been able to share her insights, ones that only someone who has lost a loved one to suicide or a devastating tragedy can truly understand. Julie became a beacon for me—a symbol of how to transform an unbearable situation into one of hope and purpose. She channeled her grief into action by organizing a Wellness Fair at our church, bringing together nonprofits focused on suicide prevention and mental health awareness. Who does that while grieving?

Julie.

I recommend Julie's book to you, whether you are helping yourself, a friend, a relative, or a colleague navigate the loss of someone to suicide, an untimely death, or any profound loss. I always tell those I counsel: You cannot cheat grief. It comes in waves, and it remains until you move through its stages and do the hard work. Julie did exactly that. She was determined to examine her grief from the underbelly of its darkest void into Heaven's light.

A Thousand Little Memories by Julie Green is the perfect book to help you understand that the end of a loved one's life is not the end of your story. It can be a new beginning.

Peace,

The Reverend Canon Cindy Evans Voorhees

Rector, St. James Episcopal Church Newport Beach, CA

I Am That Mom

I am that mom.

The mom with the story you pray every night will never be yours. The mom you look at and think, "How does she get up every morning? She is so strong." The mom that makes you hug your kids a little tighter.

I am a mom who lost a child to suicide. My son, Jack, took his life at age nineteen.

Yet, as unimaginable as it seems, I find myself able to say that I am happy—at least sometimes. I have rediscovered my capacity for happiness, for living. I can stand strong in the love I hold for my son, miss him with every fiber of my being, and still find joy in the sunrise. This unimaginable loss set me on a path of relearning how to live. By sharing my journey, I hope to guide you through your own ascent up the mountain of grief—a pilgrimage from pain and loss to healing and hope.

The death of a child is not the end of joy.

The journey I share in this book is not an easy one, but it is a story I feel compelled to tell. That journey began in the depths of despair, but it has brought me to the heights of the human spirit. I have climbed the mountain of grief and found a castle of joy in the clouds. How can the worst day, the day I lost my son, ever lead anywhere but to tragic and life-ending sorrow?

After Jack's death, I felt like a war veteran. A wounded warrior. My heart was shattered, and the pieces were riddled with battle scars. But like a Japanese kintsugi vase, the cracks in my heart have been glued back together with gold. Despite the pain of the process, my heart is stronger and more beautiful than ever. It is a work of art.

You too can become stronger through healing from grief. If you truly want to live and feel joy again in your life, there *is* a way. I am proof of that: I will never forget Jack's presence and love in my life, but my life is full. I can hold both the good and the bad together at the same time, and so can you. I truly believe that Jack would not want me to stay devastated. Neither would your loved one.

Instead, I choose to live with the happiness that Jack brought to my life while he was here. I channel his joy through me and try to give this joy to others who are in pain. My passion now is to help others through this difficult time, to show them what helped me crest the mountains of grief so they can summit them too.

According to Sean Achor, author of *The Happiness Advantage*, when a big loss occurs in your life, there are only three options to choose from.

Option 1—you can stay how you are, your mind circling in a never-ending search for why this happened.

Option 2—you can fall into a pit of self-indulgent practices to numb the pain, keeping you stuck or even leading to further harm.

Option 3—you can move through the pain, choose the path of healing, and seek ways to better yourself, ultimately discovering a deeper capacity for joy.

I chose Option 3.

I chose to move forward and upward, and I want the same for you. Picking up this book is your first step in that direction.

You are not alone. I understand your pain and devastation. I've been there. We will walk this journey together. In sharing my story, I will guide you up the mountain. You don't have to take a single step alone.

Jack's death was the worst day of my life. In some ways, *I* died that day. The part of me that was Jack's mom was suddenly taken from me. But in other ways, that day was the first day of my life. Jack's death—and the grieving process—helped me realize some pebbles of grief from my childhood that were stuck in my shoe. This version of me—the healed, happy woman who brings joy to others in their darkest moments—was born that day.

Life after loss will never be the same, but there is still joy to be found. I can't wait to show you yours.

Julie Green

Huntington Beach, CA

PART 1:
THE MOUNTAIN
OF SHOCK

Getting Through the First Phase of Grief

CHAPTER ONE

The First Day
of the Rest of My Life

I awoke at 1pm. Needing more sleep before my next shift, I popped the little pink pills. I am a nurse, and sleeping between night shifts had become harder since my son Jack was admitted to a resident psych hospital across the state. I couldn't stop worrying about him. I had gotten in the habit of taking Benadryl to be able to sleep when I needed to. That day was no different—I took the meds knowing I needed more than three hours sleep before my next shift. I glanced at my phone before trying to return to sleep when a bright voicemail notification flitted across the screen in the dark room. And somehow I knew. Even half-asleep, I could feel my intuition warning me that this was the call I'd been dreading. I immediately ran to the bathroom to make myself throw up. I had to get these pills out. I knew I needed to be fully awake for what was about to happen.

I checked my phone, and my intuition was right. Jack's facility had called. I listened to the message. A desperate voice said, "Please call me back. I have some information to relay." With trembling hands, I called the hospital where my son, my precious Jack, had been living. The same voice from the voicemail, so anxious, answered the call. She told me Jack had left the facility. This news bolted me awake. This was not good news.

She tried to explain, but I couldn't make sense of anything she was saying. How did he leave? Was he missing? Then suddenly, she cut the conversation short. New information was coming in, and she'd have to call me back. I sent Jack a text, then a second, begging him to call me. No response.

Yelling down the two flights of stairs of our tall, Victorian style home, I summoned my husband Bill and daughter Tori, quickly explaining the situation. I don't remember the minutes I spent waiting for the next call.

Next thing I knew, my family and I were in the tiny crow's nest office on the third floor, the one whose little balcony's ocean view had been my refuge during the COVID lockdown. Now, my haven held all three of us as I took the call. I turned my back to my family as I listened to each trickling piece of news.

The nurse told me Jack may have been hit by a car. I heard her words, I even repeated them back, but I just couldn't wrap my head around them. Jack was in a secure in-patient facility. He was nowhere near danger, at least not that kind. Then she told me to stay on hold for a few minutes while she got another update. My heart squeezed tight, my stomach flipped, my body seized in preparation of what I would hear next.

I turned and looked at my family. Bill leaned forward, wringing his hands, desperate not to miss a single word of information. Tori sat in the chair next to him, her innocent cherubic face scrunched up in fear of what she just heard. The woman's voice returned. I faced away once more. I could shield my family from whatever was coming, at least for a few more precious moments.

The woman told me that someone fitting Jack's description was hit by a truck on the freeway. I froze. It's amazing how quickly the brain shifts into survival mode. Mine had always been a "freeze" reaction. That coping mechanism was the best option in my early childhood trauma, and it had served me well. This day it allowed me to delay processing these terrible words, to slow my breathing so I didn't hyperventilate, to stay calm.

The news went through me to my family as I repeated her words. Somewhere far away, I could hear my husband yelling and my daughter softly crying. I was in a world apart as images of Jack ran through my head.

It's got to be a mistake, I thought. They have the wrong young man, not my Jack. Jack is fine, we will go get him when he answers my text. We'll bring him home.

The woman's voice returned, and my hopes shattered. The police had confirmed Jack's identity. They had transported him to a local trauma center, where he was in critical condition. A quick call to the hospital revealed the extent of his injuries:

blunt force trauma to his head, several fractures to his neck and spine, two collapsed lungs, a fractured pelvis, a compound fracture to his left leg, and massive internal bleeding.

The nurse on the phone made it clear: There were no guarantees, and we needed to get to the hospital ASAP. She was so calm and matter-of-fact—she was at work, reciting a list of medical terms as part of her job. I knew the tone well—I am a nurse, too, after all. But for me, the entire world hung on those cold words.

I thanked her for the information and hung up. Another amazing thing the brain does is latch onto hope no matter the odds. Despite the dismal outlook, I still hoped Jack would survive and we would be there to help support him through his recovery. He was a very strong "physical specimen," as his water polo coach would say. He had never broken a bone or needed surgery in his entire life. He was eleven pounds at birth, bruised from the speed of his delivery, so strong and full of life that he sprinted into this world. Maybe he would survive this.

Within fifteen minutes, we were out the door. The seven-hour drive felt like slow, silent torture. Each of us drifted on autopilot, lost in our own heads, thinking the worst and then battling that thought with hope. I knew the surgeons were doing everything they could to correct what a five-thousand-pound truck can inflict on the human body. But as Bill drove, I kept picturing an unrestrained test dummy in slow motion— like those I had seen in old videos on the importance of seatbelts and airbags. Except this test dummy was standing in the middle of the freeway. I fought against calling the hospital again, knowing doing so would distract my husband who had to stay focused on the road.

It felt like I was holding my breath the entire way.

Five hours into our silent journey, the doctor called. I answered and steeled myself to absorb the impact for my family if the news were bad.

"We have been working on your son for six hours straight," he said, his voice tired, "but we can't stop the bleeding." A pause, then, "He is actively dying."

I had never heard that term before. It struck me that even as his life ebbed away, Jack was actively participating, such a strange thought to have.

I remained stone-faced, betraying no emotion as I told him we were still hours away and would want to see Jack immediately when we arrived. The doctor must have thought I was in shock. It wasn't shock—it was my being the stellar soldier I had trained my whole life to be. I was saving my family from despair for a little while longer, so I couldn't react, which ripped me apart inside. I *wanted* to fall apart, to throw myself on the ground and wail uncontrollably, to scream and beg God to undo this day. But I continued the excruciatingly long trek up the highway in silence.

Darkness had fallen as we finally arrived at the hospital. COVID regulations prevented visitors, but we were immediately shepherded through the high-security hallway. Being a medical professional, I knew what that meant, but my family did not.

Jack was dead.

The medical staff greeted us in the Emergency Department before leading us to a sterile, chilly room where we waited for the doctor. My heart pounded in my ears as stoic nurses bustled about, faces hidden behind hospital masks, knowing eyes avoiding contact with us. I popped into the small hospital bathroom for a moment alone. Teal tile, a small table with urine collection containers atop, the smell of industrial-strength cleaning solution. I avoided looking into my tired eyes in the mirror's reflection. This is it, I thought. Keep it together! Just breathe. I rejoined my family, and we were escorted up to the ICU, then down low-lit empty hallways to the family conference room.

Two doctors sat facing us with six feet of space between us and them, like an invisible barrier between the ones who knew and the ones who were about to learn and be changed forever. This was a familiar scene. In my own profession, I had been the one on the other side, with the doctor relaying bad news to parents about their baby. The doctors looked worn out, like they had just completed a marathon or climbed a mountain. They described the injuries and surgeries, their words swirling around our stressed-out stupors without meaning, until one of the doctors said those dreaded words.

"He didn't make it."

Bill, my big husband with the booming voice, let out a bellow that jolted us down to our toes.

"NO! NO! NO! NOT MY SON!"

Tori sat silently in shock. Her beloved big brother, her champion since birth, her best friend—gone. I sat motionless.

The whole scenario felt so unreal, like a movie or a dream. I managed to ask a few, quickly forgotten questions, but all I really wanted was to see Jack.

The doctors looked so defeated. I know this to be the absolute worst part of their job, relaying the bad news, grating against their Hippocratic Oath to do no harm, to help people, to save lives.

They escorted us to a small room where curtains were pulled around a silent bed. The room was completely quiet, with none of the usual beeping of machines monitoring and sustaining life. Hands held tight, Bill, Tori, and I walked into the room. I took a deep breath and slowly peaked between the curtains. There he was, motionless, like a wax statue or mannequin in the hospital bed, the crisp new sheets and blanket carefully tucked up to his shoulders. Jack, my beautiful, amazing son.

Aside from a superficial scrape on the side of his nose, he looked like himself. How can this be? How can you be hit by a truck and have only one scrape on your face? It was just too impossible to make sense of.

Even with all the confusion, I felt incredibly grateful I got to see him again. I inspected him like I had the first time I saw him—nineteen years, three months, eleven days before, the moment he came into the world. He had ten fingers, ten toes. His face was the same, but his beautiful big smile was no more, and his ocean-blue eyes were closed forever.

Bill wailed in grief. Tears rolled down our cheeks as we gathered around Jack and began to hug and touch his body, his face, his hands, his ears, his neck, his chest.

How were we ever going to survive this?

After what felt like forever and yet a just flash in time, we were told the coroner was there to pick up the body. The body. That hit me. Jack was just a body. He was truly gone. I didn't have to worry about him anymore; he was dead. And in some ways so was I. I was no longer the mother of this extraordinary human who had brought so much joy into my life. We had to say goodbye. I kissed my son one last time.

I called my older boys, Jack's brothers Josh and James. They had both been with Jack in the weeks before he was admitted to the psych hospital. They were devastated. Their baby bro, who looked up to them and had shared good times so recently. Their big age gap had finally closed, and they could actually hang out as buddies.

Now he was gone.

Bill's Aunt Kit came to take us to her boyfriend Tom's condo near the hospital. She settled us in and left us to our private family grief. It had been just the four of us for so long. How would we carry on as a family? With a missing leg, our family table would surely fall over.

A big glass of wine, and another...little bites of tasteless food...tears, memories, reliving what happened over and over. I felt like I had been the one hit by a truck, an invisible truck so that no one could see my injuries. The difficulty I experienced to even get a full breath of air felt like suffocation. How could I live when my precious beautiful son was dead? How could I go on?

But I did go on. And so will you, dear friend. If you are reading this book because you lost someone, you will survive. But first, just breathe.

Breathing is such a simple act. We do it without thinking. But when bad news comes, when we are experiencing great stress, we often hold our breath. And when we do breathe again, it's shallow and rushed. That kind of breathing can lead to hyperventilation and a full-on panic attack. I found myself holding my breath as I listened to the voicemail, and again and again as bad news trickled in. All day, I kept sighing, a sign that I was not breathing deeply enough. This is not healthy for the body and brain. We need oxygen!

Breathing is the first step. Once you are breathing again, you can take my hand. You can begin to process. You can see that you are not alone.

So first, just breathe.

Try box breathing, a technique from the pranayama yoga practices that is used by Navy Seals to regulate the body under high stress. This technique is called "box breathing," because like a box, it has four sides. The exercise takes four counts of four:

1. Inhale for four counts.

2. Hold for four counts.

3. Exhale for four counts.

4. Hold again for four counts.

Repeat four times. That's it. This simple practice has been shown to lower cortisol and blood pressure, move your brain out of the "fight or flight" state, and help you regain control of your thoughts.

The recommendation is to do this several times a day, including first thing in the morning and again at the end of the day, even if you feel good. The more you practice, the longer you can stretch each "side" of the box. As you start counting to five, then six, the regulatory benefits increase. This is a powerful tool to help stop anxiety in times of stress and calm your body's response to this stress.

In the craziness of the initial news, and the chaos that follows, your mind can go numb. Mine did. I couldn't think. I actually thought I might die. Box breathing helped me regulate my nervous system enough to stay conscious. Just that little push toward control over the gargantuan emotions was enough.

Now, let's work on getting through these impossibly overwhelming initial emotions. I'll share what helped me, so you can find what works for you. Remember, you are not alone. We are in this together.

CHAPTER TWO

How the Hell
Did This Happen?

I don't remember falling asleep that first night. I woke up with swollen eyes and excruciating pain in my face from my grief-tensed muscles. Reality came crashing back in. I felt a sick falling sensation, like the earth had opened beneath me and I was no longer on solid ground. The intense worry I held for Jack over the last three months was now replaced with a dark pit in my stomach, a tightness in my throat, and a longing, aching sadness.

The earth had shifted and even the light looked different. I tried to shower—warm water cleansing my body, shampoo sudsing my hair...but it wasn't me doing it. I looked at my reflection in the mirror, and I didn't recognize the woman I saw. The self I once knew so well had died with Jack.

I was about to be thrown into a world of even deeper despair and guilt. The police called that morning to tell us what they had learned. The officer hesitated; he seemed reluctant to give this info. I don't blame him—what he said next is the last thing any mother wants to hear. He had interviewed the cargo van driver that hit Jack. Overcome with anguish, the driver could hardly tell the officer what happened. He said that Jack had run straight onto the center of the freeway, waving his arms above his head. The man had honked and tried to brake, but Jack stayed there on the road. He made eye contact with the driver just before impact. This was clearly not an accident. Jack had killed himself.

I felt so sad and guilty for what Jack had done to this poor man, forcing him into the act of ending Jack's life! I also was thrown into the never-answered question of WHY? Why would Jack do this? Why couldn't we help him? Why is this happening to us?

Jack had enjoyed a good life, one with so many advantages: a loving family, his material needs met, natural ability and charisma. He was smart, funny, loving, strong, tall, and handsome. A gifted athlete, he had been awarded a water polo scholarship to one of the best colleges in the country, University of California, Irvine. He had his girlfriend, Madi, and many great friends. He lived in the dorms at UCI, but could come home when he wanted to his supportive family only fifteen minutes away. Everything was going his way.

Or so it looked from the outside anyway.

The reality was that his magical life was unraveling so quickly that none of us realized until it was too late. A series of events and changes happened that put Jack on a trajectory toward his terrible decision.

First, Jack became disillusioned with his new water polo team. He had been one of the big stars on his high school team, but at UCI he was given "redshirt" status, which meant he could practice with the team but not participate in the games for the first season. Jack craved competition and missed the recognition. Despite not being able to play in any matches, Jack was still expected at practice every day. And he was struggling to keep up his grades. He decided to quit the team in order to concentrate on school.

I saw a change in Jack after he quit the sport. With many years of high-intensity practices two times a day, his brain craved the adrenaline and dopamine surge he got when he practiced hard and competed. Without it, he was moody and irritable. He had started recreational use of marijuana in high school (a behavior I had tried in vain to stop), and I suspected that his smoking increased in college, especially after he quit the water polo team.

Without water polo practice, Jack had more free time than he had ever had. He decided to get a part-time job and landed a great one as a valet for the impressive Lido House in Newport Beach. They told him he had "The Lido Look": tall, blonde, blue eyes, big smile, charming face—everything they wanted to represent the company. Jack loved working there. He enjoyed the lighter workload, going to parties, and just hanging out with a new group of friends.

In a few short weeks, Jack went from an over-scheduled star athlete to a casual partier. I'm sure his brain had trouble keeping up. I imagine the lack of structure and the dopamine and adrenaline withdrawals left him unbalanced. Also during this time, Jack was in a car accident. The car was totaled, but his only injury was a sore neck. Looking back, I wonder if the accident had shaken his brain. I now know that even small concussions can cause brain damage to accumulate over time.

Overall, Jack was growing more irritable, but he was still the Jack I knew: keeping up with classes, his girlfriend, and friends.

Then, COVID hit.

A mandatory shutdown at UCI was announced on March 11th, 2020, and the college dorms closed. Jack was forced to move back home and continue to go to school online. This was incredibly challenging for him. He had always struggled with Attention Deficit Disorder, having been formally diagnosed at eight years old. This made online learning nearly impossible for him. He started to lose his grounding and his confidence. Watching his decline was incredibly scary. I felt so helpless.

Bill and I agreed to allow his girlfriend, Madi, to move in with us, since her mom lived out of state and she had nowhere to go after the shutdown. Between Jack, Madi, and Tori, we now had three teenagers in lockdown in the house. We did our best to go on in these unusual circumstances.

We made food together, did puzzles, and binge-watched *Tiger King*. We celebrated Thanksgiving and Christmas at home, just the five of us. We invited the family to special events on Zoom: Jack's nineteenth birthday and Bill's sixtieth.

The days wore on, and so did the stress of the unknown. Living together became more difficult. There was thick tension in the house. As a nurse, I was still working through COVID. In fact, I picked up overtime shifts during this time, because Bill had lost his job two years prior. He had been looking for new work but hadn't found anything yet. During lockdown, the search was even harder. He was so obsessed with reclaiming his career that it took all of his focus and energy. I felt that it was up to me to keep the family going.

I was overworked by the night shifts, trying to sleep through the days with a house full of people. I felt more and more resentful but did not want to upset my perfect family. So I suppressed those angry feelings.

Bill was dealing with rejection after rejection, feeling down on himself and constantly scrolling the internet, watching TV, and looking at his phone, sometimes all at the same time. Our three teenagers tried to keep up with school on their own, caught between unhappy parents and missing what they had been promised were the best years of their lives. Each of us suppressed these feelings in order to get along.

Forced cohabitation in a rented beach house with no reprieve proved to be challenging. Jack and Madi started to argue more. They spent more time behind Jack's locked bedroom door secluding themselves. Behind that door, there was a lot of partying going. Sadly, I found out that Jack was actually selling drugs to pay for his own use.

Online school was a nightmare for Jack, but he worked hard to hide his struggle. He suggested transferring to a local junior college to save money, since he wasn't getting the benefits of UCI's high tuition online. We found out later that he was failing.

Even after the transfer, he couldn't keep up with the coursework without the structure and guidance of in-person teaching.

Over spring break, Jack and Madi drove up to Tahoe to stay with Jack's buddy from high school. They were considering staying up there for the next few months while they finished the school year. I was glad to see him wanting to reconnect with an old friend and even more happy that he would get a break from quarantine. My hope was that this trip would help him get out of his whirlwind of depression and just be happy Jack again.

I was wrong.

While on this trip, Jack and his buddy got into a wrestling match, something they often did in good spirits. But this time, their contest was fueled by drugs and alcohol, and it got out of hand. Jack hit the back of his head on a coffee table, hard enough to require a trip to the ER and six staples across the back of his head.

COVID restrictions meant no visitors could be in his hospital room nor talk to the doctors directly and get aftercare instructions. Jack suspected a concussion; he was given a CT scan, which cannot detect that type of injury. When the scan came back clear, he went right back to partying with no one looking out for him. Jack chose not to tell me or Bill about the serious injury at the time.

Jack's behavior changed after that day. Madi said that he became careless and it frightened her. She and Jack met Bill at our family cabin near Tahoe for Memorial Day, and Bill noticed a change in him too. While they were there, Jack and Madi went on a hike near the cabin that follows a little stream to a waterfall. Jack became obsessed with the idea of diving off the cliff-side trail into the tiny stream—a completely irrational idea. The danger was obvious, and no person in their right mind would think such a jump would end in anything but death. Madi had to beg Jack not to do it.

Jack had become a different person, and Madi was incredibly scared for him. Bill also mentioned that Jack was consistently angry during their stay, cursing and raising his fist in the air, ranting on and on about the friend he had wrestled. During conversations, Jack would change the subject quickly and talk so fast no one else could join the discussion. When Bill did get a word in, Jack would become enraged and bolt out of the room.

His irrational behavior became worse when he returned from Tahoe. Jack would walk into the kitchen and, again, start talking really fast—now about what he wanted to do with his future. He said he wanted to become a Muay Thai martial artist. I assumed he was desperate to find a replacement for the intensity of water polo. It seemed like a normal coping mechanism at first. But then he became obsessed.

He started worrying about his weight, something he had never focused on before. He would squeeze the roll of skin on his stomach, insisting it was fat—when he had six-pack abs. He got into a fight with Madi one day when she took a sip of the protein shake he had made, yelling that he needed to account for every calorie in his drink. He started doing strange things to strengthen his knuckles and bones, like punching the walls and rolling a stick really hard on his shins. His behavior was incredibly disturbing. When I asked why he was doing this, he would get irate and storm out of the room.

He also started ranting all the time about what was wrong in the world. I couldn't have a conversation with him. When I tried, he would get more and more agitated, talking really fast yet never finishing a train of thought. I could barely get a word in, and when I did, he would get angry and raise his fists like he was going to punch the wall. I told him I was worried about him. I begged him to get a psych evaluation, but he refused, insisting he was fine. He was an adult in the eyes of the law, so my hands were tied. I didn't want to get the police involved because I felt it would negatively affect his future in sports, school, and employment.

I was scared and overwhelmed, completely at a loss for what caused this sudden change in Jack. I hoped the situation would get better in time.

I later found out that Jack had started having paranoid delusions. One time he walked into a tattoo parlor and was denied service because the tattoo artist felt Jack was not in a good state of mind to have work done. As he was leaving the parlor, he saw a flash of light and accused the man of scanning his brain. He was convinced people were watching him. If I had known he was having these visual hallucinations, I would have demanded he get help.

Lockdown restrictions started to ease, and Jack went back to work at the Lido House. His boss noticed the change in him, and because he really liked Jack and wanted to help, moved him from valet to cleaning so he would have fewer interactions with customers. When I noticed the change in his schedule, Jack said they were preparing to make him a manager. I think he truly believed this delusion.

Then Madi went on a trip for a week, and Jack fell apart. He couldn't handle Madi not being there, claiming he needed her next to him to sleep. She later told me that, while she was gone, he became so distraught that he took a "big bag of cocaine"— one a dealer gave him to sell—and snorted it all himself.

"It's a miracle he didn't overdose that night," she said.

Jack's erratic behavior proved too much for their relationship and after two years together, they broke up. Madi moved out.

After the breakup, things got worse. I was not sure what was the cause of the behavior change or what the solution to help him really was. I offered to take him to the ER, I tried to make appointments with psychologists. I told him he needed help, someone to talk to to figure out what was wrong. He always refused. The most shocking aspect of Jack's behavior was this radical change happened in just three months. He had become an entirely different person in fewer than ninety days.

I can only imagine how scary this time was for Jack. His brain had undergone a shocking change from a perfect storm of influences. There were potential brain injuries: a hit in water polo training, the car accident, the improvised wrestling match gone awry, stitches he needed across his eyebrow after he and a friend collided playing basketball—all not fully recognized as cumulative concussions. Then there were the stressors: the loss of his sport, the family's move to a smaller home, the tense family dynamics, the pressures of being a student, the

COVID shutdown, increased drug and alcohol use, insomnia, the loss of friends' company, and isolation. Did they all trigger his brain into some sort of psychosis? Was it schizophrenia? Bipolar disorder?

His brain was in a storm, and he was probably doing everything he could think of to stabilize it or to just think straight. This makes me so sad for him, that he was suffering so much and refused to let anyone help him. He wanted so badly to appear normal again

My son James lives with his wife on a small farm in Northern California. They agreed to have Jack come work with them on their property. This seemed a perfect solution, to get Jack out of Orange County, away from all the pressures that we thought were contributing to his recent behavior change. Of course, I now know that the pressures were in his mind. It hurts me to think of how much pain Jack was in and how dangerous life had become for him. It's brutal to think I was holding everything together instead of dropping everything to help him! But at the time, a change of environment seemed like the right move.

Unfortunately, Jack's time there did not last long. Fewer than two weeks later, James said that although at first it had been great having Jack there, he couldn't stay. The reason? Jack wasn't adapting to the basic farm rules, like the animal feeding schedule. I learned the true reason later—Jack had been punching things, ranting on and on, laughing and crying at the same time when talking, causing James and his wife grave concern. They told Jack that they loved him but he needed help.

They assured him that he could return after he got help for whatever was causing his change in behavior.

Jack was expected to take the bus back home but couldn't seem to get it together to purchase a ticket or catch the ride home. He ended up staying in a rundown motel and going to the bar, where he spent all of the money he had. He was spinning out of control. I found out later that he was hanging out with drugged-out, scary people.

Out of money, Jack took a detour to a friend's house. He had an old water polo buddy who lived with his family not too far away. Jack went to his house to chill for a few days.

Jack called me to check in, and he seemed happy and more like himself. He told me not to worry about him, that he just needed a break and to be with an old friend would be good for him. The mother of Jack's friend texted me to say they were happy to have Jack stay with them, that he was welcome in their home. I was so relieved that Jack was with people who cared about him. He was going to be fine.

Then, I got the call. I was starting my shift at the hospital when I felt my phone buzzing in my pocket. It was the friend's mom calling. Anxiety rushed in. She told me they had to call the police on Jack. I couldn't catch my breath, so I sat down to focus on what she was telling me. Jack had been sitting at their dinner table when he suddenly had a change in demeanor. He was clenching his fists and looking down. She asked what was wrong.

"You want to kill me!" he blurted angrily.

Shocked at this accusation, she calmly said, "No Jack, we are trying to help you."

Then Jack got up and grabbed a sharp knife from the table. He held it out toward her and repeated, "You are trying to kill me."

They called the police. Then Jack held the knife to his own throat and threatened to kill himself. They pleaded with him to put the knife down, but he didn't. The police arrived with guns drawn and ordered him to drop the knife. He refused at first but then did let it go. He was immediately taken to the hospital.

If I had known then what I know now, I would have dropped everything to get Jack help before his erratic behavior had reached that tipping point. I had no idea at the time how truly sick Jack had become. I was operating only on what I knew at the time—his acting out in anger, a growing resentment of the world, the inability to deal with all the pressures of college from COVID lockdowns, his breaking up with Madi—these circumstances became impossible to deal with.

So many things were not in my field of awareness that I now know: the drug use, the effects from concussions, the delusions. Looking back now on all the information, it is normal to make judgments on myself. How stupid of me? How did I not see what was happening? How did I not grasp the level of his mental illness that was possessing my son?

Jack was held in the emergency room for evaluation. I was actually relieved—we were finally going to get him help, finally going to get answers! I explained to the doctor everything that

Jack had gone through—including the sudden and extreme personality changes.

An MRI showed unexplained fluid in his temporal area of the brain, but the doctor deemed it clear. I asked if this could all be from a TBI, a traumatic brain injury, but was brushed off. The medical team seemed to have their minds made up that it was strictly a psychotic break of unknown origin. I couldn't believe this was happening. Why couldn't the doctors see what I could so plainly see: Something was really wrong with Jack. But they deemed Jack's problem as simply psychotic.

So, they pumped him full of psych drugs and transferred him to an adult psychiatric facility on a short-term hold to help stabilize him.

When the short-term hold was up, he still needed help, but the options were limited. He was checked into a voluntary-stay facility. They planned to release Jack at the end of two weeks, which was their usual program. As Jack started to come out of his fog, our phone conversations became more coherent. (It's still unbelievable to me that I wasn't even allowed to see him because of COVID lockdowns.) He was actually listening to me.

I tried to reassure him that continuing treatment was the right move. He understood that what he did was serious, and he was remorseful. He was willing to stay. But then he would switch in an instant, yelling and slamming down the phone. He clearly needed long-term care and evaluation by a neurologist. Still, he could not stay where he was. The facility had its hands tied and needed Jack out after the allotted stay approved by the insurance company.

So, I looked for long-term psych care closer to home. Because the place where he was staying was not in our insurance network, they could not help with finding continuing care. One employee actually suggested a homeless shelter! My response to this was, "Are you kidding me?! My son comes from a loving family. He doesn't need a place to stay, he needs HELP!" The representative from our insurance was impossible to reach, and time was running out. I had to do all the research and networking myself. Navigating the mess of insurance coverage and referrals was a nightmare, but I eventually found a good fit with an available room.

Now all Jack needed was a referral sent from a physician in our insurance network to the new facility. That's it. A single piece of paper—signed, scanned, and emailed—was all that stood between Jack and a temporary home where he could get the help he needed.

Unfortunately, we got this news on the Friday afternoon before Labor Day weekend. By the time I got our insurance psych department on the phone, it was 3pm, and they insisted it was too late to send a same-day referral. Because of the holiday weekend, Jack's referral would have to wait until the following Tuesday.

I begged, I pleaded, I went on and on about the bed waiting for my wonderful Jack and how desperately he needed this home and this care. The new facility was available to process his admission until 7pm. Please!

NO! They flatly refused to create any more work for themselves before leaving for the holiday weekend. Jack could not be transferred until Tuesday. He would have to stay at his current facility a few extra days.

Bill and I considered bringing Jack home for the intervening days, but decided against it. We were told by experts that psych patients are much more likely to stay in treatment with a facility-to-facility transfer. We didn't want to risk Jack refusing treatment once he was home. Plus, I didn't even think I could drive him all the way home. I was afraid of him. More so, I was afraid *for* him.

Bill and I called Jack to let him know we would take him to his new facility in a few days, and he kept asking the same question over and over.

"Why can't I just come home?"

"You can't come home yet because you are still sick and need continued treatment. Dad and I want you to get better. We love you, Jack.

"Just hang in there a few more days," we said as we hung up the phone.

We didn't know at the time that would be the last conversation we had with Jack. Even with our plan, it was too late. Jack made the decision that he was going to check out... permanently.

Video surveillance from that last morning showed Jack pacing around the facility. He played some pool, ate a banana, checked his phone a few times, and then he bolted out the side door. He ran through the gate and headed to the freeway one mile from the facility—faster than anyone could stop him if they tried, though the law prevented them from doing so. They immediately called the police to report his leaving.

That last call with Jack played over and over in my head after he died. The words turned into a reel of never-ending torture. We wanted only the best for our boy. We wanted him to get the help he needed so he could come home and we could be a family again. I wanted to make him a nice dinner and sit down together at the table like we always did. I just wanted my boy back.

Most of us experience guilt after traumatic loss. We wonder if there was anything we could have done to prevent tragedy or ease suffering. It's one of those overwhelming emotions. When you lose someone to suicide, those thoughts take over. I'm sure you've gone through this too. For me, it felt like a dagger to my heart, leaving me wrecked. Today, after going through the grieving process that you're about to learn, I realize I can't take responsibility for Jack's death. It wasn't Jack who killed himself that night. It was the disease.

But which disease—drug addiction, a TBI, schizophrenia, or some other undiagnosed ailment? Whatever it was, his illness had made him a different person, someone quick to anger and easily moved by thoughts of conspiracy against him. He had clearly been battling something we didn't understand. But he had never seemed hopeless. Even when he threatened his friend and himself with the knife, he told me he was hopeful that he could manipulate them into taking him home. In treatment, he seemed like he wanted to get out, not end it all.

When had he given up?

It is obvious now that his brain was not functioning properly—his brain had a wounded neuro system, causing him to make decisions that made no sense but seemed right to him at that time. These reasons for the change in his thinking and the desire to take his life might have been detected but it happened so fast that it was difficult to act on. The choices he made were out of my control. He was an adult in the eyes of the law, so my rights as a parent were limited in helping him. Even if I could have helped more, I'm not sure doing so would have changed the outcome.

I began searching my memory for any indication that he had this plan in place. The guilt was overwhelming. Why did I not stop this from happening, how did I not know? This is a common reaction after someone dies; the brain wants answers but sometimes there are none.

It is important to accept that their decision to end their life was out of your control. Even if you had all the information, there was no magical right thing you could have said to take that option away. This is an imperfect world where sometimes horrors happen.

I started thinking, maybe I did know what Jack was planning. I started questioning myself. Did I ignore the obvious? Was I a monster?

I felt like I was losing my mind, *because I was*—at least for a segment of time. I believe, when you lose your son or any loved one, you do lose your mind.

This extreme guilt feels like insanity. These thoughts dominated my waking hours and caused me to have such a high stress response that *my* brain was flooded with chemicals that affect the entire body but especially the brain. Research shows that increased cortisol after a loss contributes to disturbances in how the brain functions and puts you in a fight or flight response that feels like panic. You naturally want to fix what is creating this panic but this is difficult when there are no answers and you find you cannot resolve the problem.

The first step in changing this panic response is finding meaning for the loss. This can be found by participating in rituals. I will show you how rituals helped me in my journey to heal and how creating your own can play a vital role in your journey on this first mountain.

CHAPTER THREE

The Rituals

Bill and I agreed to drive out to the place where Jack was hit. I just had to go see it. We got the exact location from the police officer. Tori, my best friend Beth and her daughter Olivia, and other family members came with us. We were a three-car procession: a little tribe mourning together.

When we arrived, we placed a sign with the words "LOVED ALWAYS JACK," several framed photos, and some silk flowers in pots. Traffic whizzed by, sucking us toward the street and filling our heads with a deafening roar. It felt so vulnerable to be out there, so exposed and dangerous. I imagined how those final minutes must have felt for Jack. As he hovered at the edge of the freeway, about to run straight out into traffic, choosing a vehicle that would ensure the end for himself. I was oddly moved; how did he move forward with this action when it was so terrifying? Here I was, standing where he stood on the side of the road, a metaphorical cliff's edge. Would I jump too? The thought scared me. I stepped back from the road and joined my family in the car.

While I felt like I floated through the experience, unsure whether I was standing next to the highway or a tear-streaked stranger, the mini memorial was one of the first and most impactful rituals I experienced. As I said earlier, rituals are the first step in reducing the panic feeling that accompanies loss. You may not find any meaning to the loss in these first steps, but performing these little rituals moves you in the direction of healing.

We stopped by the psychiatric hospital the next day to collect Jack's belongings, then flew home. That's when the flood of friends and family began. Over the next week, a casserole train rolled through our kitchen, and flowers filled the long mahogany table in our dining room. That was the one where we had family dinners and celebrations. During COVID, it became our puzzle table. Now it was a memorial site.

Then the rituals began. We started funeral preparations, and a million little decisions had to be made. Jack's grandparents, his brothers, his girlfriend, and countless friends deserved a chance to say goodbye. Plus, I wanted to see my Jack one last time. Cesar Gutierrez of The Heritage Memorial Funeral Home in Huntington Beach, one of the most kind, thoughtful, and compassionate men I have ever met, personally drove Jack back to Southern California.

He said that he wanted to—he had a nineteen-year-old son of his own. Cesar arranged a small viewing for us at his funeral home.

Dressed in his favorite jeans, white sweatshirt, and Adidas, Jack looked like Sleeping Beauty. The coveted gray tiger-print blanket, one I gave him years ago, was placed over him. He looked peaceful but empty. A shell. He had always been filled with love, talent, laughter, and so much more, but this was just the empty vessel.

After the viewing, Bill and I took a few minutes alone with Jack. We told him how proud we were to be his parents, and we sang a lullaby from my childhood that I always sang to my babies. It was how we would get Jack to stop crying and go to sleep. That day, we sang it one last time for Jack's final eternal rest.

"Sail, baby, sail, out across the sea, only don't forget to sail home again to me."

We shook with great sobs as we gave Jack a final hug goodbye. I took the blanket home with me; it still smelled like Jack.

The next important ritual was performed by Jack's friends. They decided to do a "paddle out." This Hawaiian tradition has been adopted in the beach cities, especially among the surfing community. Surfers paddle into the ocean on their boards with flowers and leaves around their necks or between their teeth and join hands to form a floating circle. One or more people offer words of remembrance about the departed. Then the whole party erupts in hoots and cheers, splashes the water, and throws the flowers into the air.

Jack was a big-time water polo player, and his best friends were all Huntington Beach water babies raised in the Pacific. This paddle out was organized by my oldest son, who grew up in Huntington Beach and understood the importance of this ritual for Jack's friends. Over one hundred people filled the beach that blustery September evening. One by one, then in groups, the strong young men and women grabbed a single white rose from the bucket we provided. The surf was very rough, but they braved the tumultuous waves to paddle past the break to calmer water. The aerial picture of the ocean taken with a drone shows everyone in formation, but instead of a circle, the unplanned shape of a heart emerged. One of Jack's good friends told me later that his closest friends each got to go to the middle and speak. I wish I could have heard their words, but the ritual was beautiful and intimate—just them, a sacred ceremony for their buddy.

Bill and I watched them circle up from the shore, as did about half the people there to say goodbye. Bill and I moved to a spot on the beach away from everyone else. I felt so alone in my grief, like I was a ghost—the ghost of Water Polo Mom Past. Many of the other team parents were there that day, all watching from the shore as their sons said goodbye to their beloved teammate. They were the same parents Bill and I had spent many hours with at poolside, cheering on the boys. We became a little family. We all knew well what it took to get a kid into a Division 1 school: a village. I realized that this role I had played for all those years was gone. My identity as a team mom was dead, gone forever. This realization made me feel even more alone, even with Jack's dad by my side.

Next came the official funeral with smaller rituals of its own—it was a formal event after all. Clothes, hair, nails…how does one decide what to wear to your son's funeral? I picked the black silk dress I purchased for my Italy trip with Jack in 2018. I had worn it on our grand finale night in Rome. Memories of that trip got me through a lot of rough times; hopefully the dress would help carry me through today. My hair stylist made small talk as I teetered between a perfunctory "I'm fine" and gushing my grief all over his salon floor.

The nail appointment was not my usual. As a nurse I have to keep my nails short with no polish. but I wanted to share this girl ritual with Tori and Jack's girlfriend, Madi. I wanted a way to pamper them. It was grounding to have that time together before the funeral. We were our own little island, isolated amongst nail techs whose language we couldn't speak and who had no idea we were getting ready for a funeral. The three of us exchanged looks with the shared understanding of the absurdity of the situation. We were trying to do something normal when everything we knew in the world had gone crazy. I found myself looking for distractions from the overwhelming grief: the TV on the wall, the little statue of Buddha, the sharp smell of acetone, the soft towel under my hands. For a moment, I could pull my mind back from the sadness. A refuge in my storm of pain.

The funeral was held at St. James Episcopal Church in Newport Beach. The night before, Bill and I had brought Jack's ashes from the funeral home to the church. Bill had carried the surprisingly heavy box of ashes tenderly, like he used to when Jack was a baby, a cruel facsimile of such a familiar feeling. We placed the box on a pedestal at the front of the sanctuary and covered it in a white cloth for his night of repose, another small ritual of respect. The next day, we arrived at the church in our black Sunday best.

COVID funerals were different. The mask mandate, reluctance to be within six feet of each other, hesitance to hug. Regulations meant only a select number of attendees, and the masks made it hard for me to even know who some of the people were. Our wonderful friend Jim delivered the eulogy. He had known Jack from birth. Jim told everyone to "live like Jack, be Jack, walk into a room with a big smile, include others and make them feel welcome, like Jack did." We all felt inspired by his words. Next, one of Jack's friends played a touching tribute song he had written when he first heard the news. The reverend prayed over his ashes, and then this important piece of Jack's passing was over. Jack's funeral was the most beautiful and meaningful service I have ever been to.

Until I watched the video months later, the details of the funeral were a blur, muddled by my all-consuming grief, but the feeling it gave me cut through the fog. That I remember clearly. I felt unfathomably deep sorrow, warm gratitude, and pride. Jack's life was being honored in the best way possible, and that meant everything to me. In honoring Jack, I was also honoring myself as the mother of this beautiful human that God had blessed me with for nineteen years. This was a celebration for all the things we gave him as his family and for all that I gave him as his mom. Jack's death had also been mine, the death of my role as his mother. The funeral allowed me to feel the chasm of loss and the hope of rebirth. It was the first time since the horrible phone call that I had felt warm and comforted.

Immediately after the service, Jack's ashes were prepared for internment. Only the immediate family and Madi were in attendance to put his ashes into their final resting place. The tiny brass door was closed and locked shut with special screws. Suddenly, the ritual was over. We were left looking at an inscribed plaque on a wall. It was difficult to see his name on that plaque, yet I was relieved his ashes were in a safe place. I still felt the need to protect him. It was gut-wrenching and soothing at the same time. My fingers traced the letter on the brass plate, so hard and cold to the touch. With tears streaking down my face, I kissed him goodbye once more. Besides photos of Jack, this small plaque was the only remaining evidence that he existed in the physical form.

My parents graciously offered their backyard for a memorial gathering after the funeral. As nice as it was, somehow the reception left me feeling empty. I felt like time was racing and I couldn't catch up, like a dream when you are chasing something that remains just out of reach. I wanted more of Jack's friends to speak, so I could hear fun stories of his life and his relationships. I wanted to keep celebrating Jack, to lift up his memory. It seemed like everyone was sitting motionless and I was racing around, trying to connect to every single guest and hear every unique story. Impossible.

That evening, we had a house full of guests: my two older sons, Josh and James, my cousin and her fiancé, and a good friend from Napa. My parents, some close friends, Madi, and many of Jack's friends came over too. We ordered pizza, and the friend group partied on the rooftop patio until the wee hours of the morning. They celebrated Jack in their own tribal way. It was so comforting to have them all there, telling stories and laughing. I stayed up most of the night, sitting between my two oldest on the sofa after the house was quiet, laughing through tears at their funny way of brotherly jousting. I was so grateful to have them there with me that night.

Some rituals are unexpected and miraculously created. The first surprise occurred for me the day after Jack's funeral. We were in my parents' yard helping clean up from the reception gathering. A beautiful dragonfly, an iridescent bluish-green with clear cellophane wings, flew from one side of the tree-lined yard and stopped directly in front of me. I swear he looked right into my eyes. He then flew to the other side of the yard and back, again stopping to look into my eyes, then repeated this three times. My heart jumped for joy, as this felt like a sign from Jack. Or was it Jack's spirit in this mythical insect? Either way, it made me feel that Jack was still with me, all around me. I was not alone.

Those first few weeks were filled with rituals—some somber and devastating, some playful and uplifting. Each one brought new context to my sorrow and new perspectives on how special Jack really was. They were my first heart-wrenching steps toward healing. Rituals around death are so important. We have realized this even more with the inability to have important ceremonies during the COVID pandemic.

You may not want a religious ceremony or any kind of large event, and that's perfectly okay. You should never feel pressured to do anything that doesn't resonate with you. However, I encourage you to find a small ritual to bring meaning to your loss—something that honors the relationship you shared and helps you say goodbye. A ritual that grounds you in the reality that your loved one is no longer physically present. I assure you, this is essential.

Even small rituals can help, like the ones I used without even knowing, but now recognize as grounding techniques. In my story, you may have noticed my enduring the moments of overwhelm by focusing on a smell or tactile texture. I also found peace in funny stories about Jack and reciting rhymes from his childhood. Grounding rituals like these may help you focus on the present moment and distract yourself from insurmountable thoughts and feelings. They're especially helpful for improving many of the symptoms of grief: anxiety, stress, depression, post-traumatic stress disorder, and dissociation.

Some of my favorite mini rituals to ground myself are washing my hands in warm then cold water, taking a walk, and visualizing a rote daily task I like doing. (For me, it's laundry. Crazy, I know.) I find these small rituals comforting, and they make me feel like me again. There are also many techniques that use awareness of your senses to connect you to your body, such as naming things you can feel, hear, or smell. You can also hone in on how different parts of your body feel or on one particular sensation, such as how your food tastes. I also like mental grounding techniques, like repeating a common phrase or counting backwards from one hundred. All of these exercises serve to distract you from whatever is putting your nervous system on alert and help you feel in control and yourself again.

I also found myself making new rituals—patterns I could fall back on when I needed to escape the heavy emotions. It's okay to want to stay numb! It's a trauma response for a reason. In the weeks after Jack's death, I would spend hours binging on Netflix, watching the flames of my candles or fireplace dance, coloring, scrolling Pinterest. These became rituals too. They didn't take me back to myself, but they helped create the necessary distance from the grief to get through the day.

In the early weeks, such simple, almost meaningless rituals can be enough.

Some rituals become something you will want to do each year. I encourage you to continue to honor your loved one through new traditions that bring the memory back in a positive way. Jack loved our Christmas celebrations, and the first Christmas after he passed, I put a big picture of him on one of the dining room chairs. We set a place at the table for him. He was in all of our Christmas morning and Christmas dinner pictures. Jack's place at the table is now one of our core holiday experiences.

On Jack's birthday, April 16th, Tori and I decided to visit Disneyland in memory of all the fun we shared there. This also became an annual tradition. I love this trip—such a sweet reminder of the joy of Jack's life. This past year, I was in Florida in April, and Tori and I still found a way to keep the tradition alive. I visited Disney World as Tori and a friend visited Disneyland. We met on Facetime to raise a toast to Jack.

You will find your own ways of remembering and honoring your deceased. It makes me sad to hear of people deciding to stop celebrating anything now that the person is no longer here. I think that our loved ones would want us to be happy, to remember the wonderful times we had with them, and to start new traditions that can include them in a special way. It may be too difficult for you to continue the same traditions, and that is okay. But don't just put the memory away. Find a new way to include your lost loved one and create something meaningful for you.

While these rituals helped me to weather the storm of emotions surging inside me, there were moments when I wanted to drown in them. After the initial funeral services and gathering at our home, and everyone returned to their own lives, I could have easily found the dark hole, crawl in, and never come out. Luckily, that's not what I did. I found strength in the rituals. This strength gave way to hope. I couldn't imagine ever being okay or feeling like myself again, but I began to be capable of hoping I could.

In the next chapter, you will learn how small glimpses of hope can grow into mighty acts of courage.

CHAPTER FOUR

Glimpses of Hope

The whirlwind of events leading up to Jack's funeral kept me on a merry-go-round of emotions. But afterward, my mind was in a different place. I kept replaying the final hours of my last contact with Jack over and over on a loop. My mind was trying desperately to make some sense of the senseless; if I could just figure it out, maybe the outcome would be different.

This normal phase of grief is shock—sometimes confused with what is explained as the denial stage in Kubler-Ross's five stages of grief. (The Kubler-Ross stages were meant for someone experiencing grief over a terminal illness, not a death.) I didn't deny what happened: I knew Jack was dead. I saw him with my own eyes, touched his cold skin, kissed his cheek one last time. There was no denial of this fact. What I experienced was possibly a denial of the full impact, a defense mechanism the brain goes into for a person to be able to function and not completely fall apart in the immediate time following a big loss.

My shock was deepened by guilt. It is common for survivors of loss, and especially loss by suicide, to search for the single fork in the road that would have magically led to a future where our loved one lives. I replayed countless moments from Jack's life, looking for the memory that proved his death was my fault.

Could I have prevented this if I had noticed his personality changes sooner? What if I had insisted on a mental health facility closer to home? Maybe my blame went further back. Did we tell him he was Olympic material one too many times? Send him to the wrong college? Maybe it was our move to Napa at age five that set him in this direction, or the day we started medicating his ADHD.

I even found myself crying over his circumcision, convinced that a different choice would have put him on a better path from the beginning. Circumcision! I had truly convinced myself that every parenting choice from the last two decades warranted examination. Any one of them could have been the fatal blow. I felt the weight of being somehow single-handedly responsible for his ultimate decision. If I could just figure out how that could be true, at least his suicide would make sense.

That's what the brain does when confronted with unpredictable, uncontrollable calamity. It tries to make sense of the senseless.

If you find yourself in a constant loop replaying events, it's okay. You are normal. Do not judge yourself; your brain is just trying to make the unthinkable make sense. Just recognize the pattern of this behavior loop and do your best to let it go. I will share with you later in this book how I stopped this pattern in hopes my experience will help you on your journey to recovery from grief.

I started to realize that this thinking was poisoning my brain, keeping me in a circle of sadness where I saw Jack's life only through the prism of his last three months, along with my failure as a mom. But this was not true. I was a good mom. I did everything possible to have a healthy baby even before I got pregnant. Jack's was a much-wanted pregnancy, and I was an older, wiser mom, ready for all that a new baby would bring. I breastfed and took excellent care of myself and Jack, bought the *Baby Einstein* tapes, chose organic baby food—the whole package. Every detail from the start was focused on his health and happiness. I also know I was a good mom because he always knew how much I loved him. He wrote it in every card he gave me. I still have them all.

I needed to look at Jack's life in full, not just the last devastating months. The reality is that Jack had an awesome life. He was happy most of the time and had a good relationship with me and the whole family. I started to shift my thinking to focus on these good times as much as possible. I would allow myself times of sadness but not let them continue for too long. You can shift your thinking; it is a technique that I will share more of in subsequent chapters. I still work on this every day.

Learning about grief helped me make that shift. As a nurse, I was well aware of what physical shock does to the body. I knew that emotional shock can produce the same symptoms. It floods our bodies with adrenaline and other stress hormones, which overtax our entire system. We make and pump as much adrenaline as we can, then collapse. In grief recovery, this is called "crisis fatigue." The physical symptoms of extreme stress literally tire out the body. At this stage, you need rest. Physical, mental, and emotional. It's okay to take the most bereavement leave you can. It's okay to stay numb and let your body recuperate its hormones and neurotransmitters. It's okay to sleep.

The best part about this phase of climbing the mountain of shock is that other people will step up to help you. Let them.

The worst part is…that other people will step up to help you, but not always in ways you need or want. But just let them.

We were sent so many beautiful flowers after Jack died that our front room looked like a mini mausoleum. This part of our house became gorgeous, sacred, full of love…but unusable. Flower arrangements and more surrounded us—vases, sympathy cards, a white rose wreath, a silk banner with his name written in glitter.

Gratitude for the outpouring of support does not even begin to express how it made us feel. Each vase was a statement of love from someone who helped us walk through the death rituals that gave our grief some peace, and the act of sending flowers was people's own ritual for saying goodbye to Jack and supporting us as best they could. Like we talked about in the previous chapter, rituals after a death can be comforting. They give our grief some context and give the community a structure to rally around. But some rituals can be paralyzing, especially when overdone. Flowers, food, and visiting seem to be universal signs of support for the grieving, and although much appreciated, they can be overwhelming.

My house started to feel like a flower-ringed grief museum.

Then the flowers began to break down. Petals fell onto the table as once-beautiful blooms wilted. Vases turned greenish brown as water turned to slime. The smell started to take over. We were already overwhelmed by the volume of flowers coming in, and then the foliage turned into a decaying swamp. It was a second death, one that physically surrounded us. So many loved ones gifted beautiful flowers with the best intentions, but the arrangements overtook our lives and brought more death into our home.

Then my sweet cousin suggested we redo all of the flowers to freshen the room. We removed the dead ones, cut the rotten ends, and replaced the murky water. Such a caring gesture and one that gave me something productive to do. I ended up doing this several more times over the next week. It felt good to have a project to get my mind off my sadness for a short time. I also removed the white satin sash from Jack's wreath and placed it in my china cabinet.

Still, the flowers kept dying. The purges became more frequent, and they started to inspire guilt. I hated throwing them away—even the dilapidated wreath, missing its sash and sprinkling crunchy refuse onto the floor each day. I would quickly gather the discards like a mother duck gathering her babies, sweeping around to not miss a petal or twig. Yet I just couldn't throw them away. Later I placed all the dried flowers from the wreath into a decorative jar as a keepsake.

People just want to do something to comfort you during this difficult time, but there are limited ways to show that concern. Most people, including myself, usually turn to one of the learned societal norms of showing concern and sympathy: flowers and cards, food and drinks. These items did make me feel better as they were outward symbols of others' deep emotions and support for our loss. It was comforting to know so many people cared. But when the flowers died, I mourned even harder.

Another popular support gift was a tree planted in Jack's name. Several people gave certificates stating a tree for Jack would be planted in a forest somewhere, similar to buying a star to be named. I loved this idea, but it was so intangible. I wished I could know the exact tree so I could visit and hug Jack's tree. I felt a little sad that I couldn't.

With the flowers came food—so much food! I was fortunate to receive meals from Jack's water polo community and my church, and my work colleagues set up a meal train. Meals were dropped off around 5pm for two weeks. Knowing there would be hot dinner available for my family and extra leftovers for lunch the next day was amazingly comforting. This type of support is wonderful to get through those initial difficult weeks. We received tray after tray of Mexican and Italian food, clearly the go-to comfort food in SoCal. I can only imagine the types of comfort food donations in other parts of the country. What an interesting cookbook *Food for the Mourning* would be.

Even though these contributions were sweet and much appreciated, we were overrun with food. Organizing our fridge became a job. I gave away bags of food to friends. I kept having to turn away loved ones who offered to cook in our home. What I also really needed was tangible, helpful essentials: toilet paper, a basket of snacks, napkins, paper plates, Kleenex, plastic utensils, and water bottles. (One thoughtful friend supplied all of this.) I set food, utensils, plates, napkins, etc., on the counter, a makeshift command center for eating. We had people in and out for days on end, and this "buffet" made it easy for everyone to help themselves.

One time, a church member dropped off a hot-and-ready meal just as friends were arriving with dinner. I felt so guilty! Like I was taking advantage of my community by getting too much food. I had to learn to accept charity without that guilt. I sometimes had to pretend to be happy and appear strong even when all I wanted to do was disappear to my bed. But I also didn't want to offend anyone trying to help us. What I did do was thank the church member for her kindness and decide I didn't need to explain. This guilt was all in my imagination; no one was judging me. I realized I was being cared for and accepted the love for what it was. I learned that I didn't have to put up a fake front for others.

Unfortunately, sometimes the food came with caring friends who wanted to spend time with us at the wrong moment.

I love these people. They were Jack's friends, my friends, our family, our church. I wanted so badly to connect. But sometimes I would be crying, alone with my grief, and then find myself jumping up to entertain at the sound of the doorbell.

My advice for the grieving is to be clear with your community about what types of food would be most welcome and helpful, by communicating to the person who is organizing any donations. Food prepared by a local restaurant was what

I liked best, delivered at dinner time, hot and ready to go. I know I gave away several dishes that required cooking and some experimental concoctions made by more adventurous eaters than our family. I also recommend setting up a cooler outside the front door with a note attached saying not to disturb the family in mourning. This gives the family privacy in case a vulnerable moment coincides with meal drop-off. Even though I was always thankful, I would have appreciated not having to show the thankful face.

In addition to flowers and food, we had a steady stream of visitors moving through. We loved the outpouring of support, especially the friends who always texted first. I had one friend who brought my favorite Starbucks drink by the house every morning that first week. It was such a sweet gesture and the perfect amount of in-person support. But, like the other rituals around grief support, too many or too-intense visits were common. I did encounter some acquaintances who wanted to come over to commiserate about tragedy. They would tell me the entire story of their own loss. I wanted to connect with these people, but I just didn't have the capacity to comfort anyone else.

My family also experienced many well-wishers who were moved by Jack's suicide to wrestle with their own beliefs about spirituality and the afterlife. They would often say Jack was "in a better place." These interactions drained so much of our already-stretched energy.

Bill in particular was very sensitive to this. He once confronted a friend who said this with "I don't believe that. The better place is here with us." When she insisted that Jack was with God and suggested that was better than being alive, Bill lost it. He yelled at her to "Shut the f*** up!" The friendship never recovered.

A well-meaning coworker said similar things to me during my very first shift after my month-long bereavement leave, then doubled down when I told him his words were not helpful. Many people used the phrase "committed suicide," which is hurtful language left over from a time when suicide was considered a crime. If I gently corrected people that Jack "*died* by suicide," some would insist that he had committed a spiritual crime. One woman even suggested that Jack's suicide could have been brought on by a vitamin B deficiency.

Something I kept hearing was "You are so strong." This is such a common and well-meant phrase. I have said it too. It seems like an encouraging compliment. But when my grief was fresh, I felt anything but strong. When people said this, it made me feel like I *had* to be strong. I couldn't let down the people who did so much to support me. But pretending to be strong was exhausting.

As a society we are afraid to see people show emotion. We try to comfort our friends by stopping their tears. We put our hand on a shoulder, hand them a tissue, and tell them they are strong. These actions stop the emotion from being expressed. But the kindest thing we can do for a grieving person is allow them to emote without stopping it, to show them they can still be loved and you are willing to be present while they cry. It can feel uncomfortable to see someone cry and to just allow that to happen. Showing concern through facial expressions and nonverbal actions, communicating "I am here for you and I'm not going anywhere" is most helpful. No words needed. Just a big hug and offer of tissues when they are ready. Be present and allow the tears to flow uninterrupted.

It is okay to not be strong. You are in pain, your heart is broken, and you need to heal that schism in order to recover. The way to heal your heart begins with accessing the painful emotions and letting them out through tears and other expressions. Bottling up these emotions to seem strong can lead to depression and other illnesses. But daring to feel your grief? That's true strength.

It's okay to say the wrong thing to these friends and for them to say the wrong thing to you. I know that everyone whose words stung would never have said them if they knew they would be hurtful. Words spoken when trying to comfort someone in grief all came from a loving place, and I give them grace for even trying to comfort us in our darkest hour. I love them for trying. But when my grief was fresh, I did not have the emotional energy for morality debates or someone else's tragedy. The best way for me to receive support was a simple "I don't know what to say, but I am so saddened by what you are going through." Some sweet people knew that just being there, present, no words needed, seeing needs and just doing them without being asked, was the most helpful support of all.

In the first few weeks after Jack's death, my family was amazingly well supported. We are so lucky to have so many truly generous, compassionate people in our community. The majority of our army of supporters did or said exactly the right thing, even in ways we couldn't articulate. The few who overwhelmed us with excessive gifts, food, and conversation did so out of love, and most of them were very open to supporting in different ways when asked. We had much to be grateful for.

Still, we didn't always see that. We also said the wrong things. Bill and I both yelled at each other and our family when we didn't have to and plastered fake smiles on our faces to thank people for stopping by when we wanted to be alone. It was a difficult and awkward time. We were thrown into an unknown realm with no blueprint for how to act. I hope that by sharing some of my experiences, I can help you see that it's okay to mess up in grief. Give yourself grace for your reactions to people saying or doing the wrong thing.

You don't have to live in the decaying mess of well-meant floral arrangements. You might think you will hurt someone's feelings, but it's still okay to toss those flowers. The people who sent them did so in a gesture of love and support because they really don't know what else to do. Hopefully, in time, more people will understand grief better and change old beliefs, acts, and words we were all taught about comforting the grieving. Standing up for yourself, even if you don't do it "right," is part of that learning.

I wish I had stood up for myself more. I truly think healing would have been easier if I had said no to the things I did not want. At the very least, I wish I had not let myself feel guilty for tossing the damn flowers. I had enough groundless guilt on my shoulders already.

As I shared earlier, examining that guilt led me to view Jack's life as whole. I'm so grateful for that painful misplaced guilt. It forced me to evaluate Jack's life and my role in it in full context, and letting go of that guilt opened the door to hope. I could be proud of the life I gave him. I was still suffocating under the weight of despair, but I began to hope that I might one day be myself again. The definition of hope, and the following reading from my daily devotional, gave me inspiration and helped me start the journey.

Hope: a desire of some good, accompanied with at least a slight expectation of obtaining it, or a belief that it is obtainable. Hope differs from wish and desire in that it implies some expectation of obtaining the good desired. Hope therefore always gives pleasure or joy.

KJV Dictionary

Hope always looks to the future; it's always on tiptoes, leaning forward.
It keeps us going. It makes a dismal today bearable because it promises a brighter tomorrow. Without hope, something inside all of us dies.

Wisdom for the Way daily devotional

To hope is to anticipate. It is more than dreaming; it is possessing within ourselves an expectation that someday there will be the fulfillment of that desire. It will become a reality.

We can live several weeks without food, days without water, and only minutes without oxygen, but without hope—forget it. I had gotten through the shock of the initial loss, and I was ready to follow the glimmer of hope within me. Join me as we start climbing the Mountain of Hope.

PART 2: THE MOUNTAIN OF HOPE

The Beginning of Healing

CHAPTER FIVE

The Glimmer

A few weeks after Jack's death, Tori and I were having coffee in the kitchen. We had talked about Jack so much over the last month that we'd reached an exhausted quietness. We just sat together, sharing our coffee and home and silent support. Suddenly, she turned to me.

"I'm afraid to have a son one day," she whispered. "The men in our family are cursed."

Our family's continued misfortune did feel like a curse. My biological father, Jim, my brother Jimmy, my son Jack— all battled mental illness and addiction, all gone too young. I remembered thinking we were cursed after Jimmy's death decades ago. I had been Tori's age, and Jimmy had been nineteen, like Jack. Talk about déjà vu. I had expressed that fear to my own mom: Why do our men keep dying?

My mom had never given me an answer. She didn't know how to process her grief, so she buried it under layers of shame. When I was growing up, no one talked about anything serious in my family. We were taught to keep our feelings bottled up inside so we wouldn't upset our mother's fragile state. It felt like she was always on the verge of a nervous breakdown. When Jimmy died, she had no support. She had to walk through the aftermath of losing her son all alone. The fact that she is now doing quite well is a miracle.

I stirred out of my reverie, and there was Tori waiting for a reply, fear in her eyes. I felt like I was looking at my own teenage self. My mom hadn't been able to comfort me or talk about my fears. But I could. I could end my family's cycle of shame.

I smiled. "Well, if our family is cursed, it must be a biblical curse, and in the Bible I think curses last three generations, so your kids will be in the clear."

I paused. Slowly, Tori smiled back. It wasn't a joke per se. Neither of us was ready for jokes yet. But it was silly, and the idea lightened the mood. And it gave her hope.

I leaned in and put my hand on her arm.

"We're not cursed, Tori. Bad things happen sometimes. But whatever happens, we can work through it. If we've had three generations of tragedy, we've also had three generations of incredibly strong women who have kept the family together through it all. We're a family of women warriors, and we'll be okay. It would be a great joy to be a grandmother to your children one day, whoever they are."

That's the power of hope. I found myself dreaming not only of my own healing, but of Tori's. If I could hope for myself, I could hope for the family. I could break intergenerational curses. I could set us free.

I started with my own healing. Baby steps. Literally. I went for walks.

I met up with friends, got a coffee, and talked. I used the time to connect and vent, and that helped in its own way. But the first shift toward healing came from walking itself. Physical activity promotes release of brain chemicals such as endorphins to help relieve emotional discomfort. Exercise can help a person regulate their mood and keep their grief from growing into depression. Movement also tells our bodies that we are okay. We are alive. We want to live. If walking doesn't feel good for you, pick another movement. Any movement, even just swinging your arms around and twisting your body side to side, will help your brain readjust the grief cocktail of emotion chemicals to a healthy balance.

Even the smallest hint to your body that it is still alive can help you start to process your emotions. The body wants to get back in balance, to regulate those emotion chemicals, to heal. Sometimes it just needs a wake-up call.

Without that little reminder, you can stay numb for years. Just like my cousin Laura…she waited years to truly process her grief and is just willing to do so now.

Laura and her husband, Roman, lost their precious son, Danny, to a rare childhood cancer, rhabdomyosarcoma, in 2008. He was seventeen. He was diagnosed on April 6th, 2007, which happened to be Good Friday, and lived eighteen months before succumbing to the insidious disease.

Danny was an outgoing, athletic teenager with many friends. He included everyone he met, especially befriending new kids at school and making them feel welcome. Just a sweet soul. When Danny was diagnosed, his friends supported him through his illness. For the first three years after Danny died, his friends created an event to memorialize him, a fundraiser they called Dannypalooza. This fun community event raised money for other families going through cancer treatment.

Laura agreed to an interview to help me write this book. It's hard to believe, but the day we did the interview was one day before the fifteenth anniversary of Danny's death. I know, in doing this interview, Laura felt some relief talking about Danny, reliving the raw emotions with the details of his passing, something she said she hasn't completely processed even now. This is common; most people don't want to face this pain. Maybe you also have not processed your loss.

When Laura first heard Danny's diagnosis, she fell to her knees and begged God, "No! Don't let this be true!" When she read the paperwork describing the disease, diffusely metastasized, she couldn't breathe. She just couldn't believe the cancer had spread all over his body so quickly. Even in our interview, Laura said she still sometimes can't believe this happened, that she can see it in her head but can't feel it. Remembering that day is like watching a dream or a movie showing someone else's experience. The brain does this to protect us from the shock, but eventually the shock goes away and reality sinks in. And with that reality comes pain. Feeling pain is a necessary part of processing grief.

Laura said she spent her time after Danny died either numbing the pain or making plans to numb the pain. She drank. A lot. She drank every night and stayed so busy with work that she didn't have time to think about the loss of Danny. These were her most effective coping mechanisms. She had terrible insomnia as well, another common symptom of grief, especially after the loss of a child. When we go to bed, there are no distractions, so the brain races with thoughts of the loss. Laura took sleeping pills prescribed by her doctor to help her. She said this was the hardest habit to break.

Both Laura and Roman threw themselves into their restaurant and baking business, staying too busy to confront the pain of their son's death. They seized every opportunity to expand, knowing it would distract them from the harsh reality. But as they buried themselves in work, their marriage began to suffer. Despite years of a strong partnership, this loss tested their relationship in ways they weren't sure they could survive. They found themselves blaming each other for decisions about Danny's end-of-life care they hadn't agreed on. This is a common reaction—anger, often more powerful than grief, can take over when we're unwilling to face the deeper pain.

Their confrontations became so frequent and heated that Roman asked Laura if she wanted a divorce. At first she said, "Deal. It would make my life a lot easier."

But then Roman paused. "Is that what you really want?"

Laura was quiet for a while. As she sat there in silence all she could think was, No, I don't want a divorce.

And they left it at that.

Over the years their marriage got better. I started seeing evidence of their being together and happy, smiling at the camera when they visited their older son in New York, taking trips with friends. I recently saw Laura and Roman in San Francisco at a family wedding for our youngest first cousin. It had been a while, and this was the first time being around many of my relatives since Jack had passed. I asked Laura what shifted in her marriage to be seemingly happy now. She told me she decided to forgive Roman and to just love him. So simple to make that decision, but it changed everything for them.

In our interview, Laura realized that she, fifteen years after losing Danny, has still not dealt with her grief. And now she is ready. She is ready to feel the pain and do the work to process that grief. She doesn't want to numb the pain any longer because she realizes taking that step is the only way to process the grief of her loss. She told me she isn't sure she can feel the pain now, because she has numbed it for so long. I gave her hope in what helped me. I sent her all of my resources, which I will also share in this book, to help anyone in this situation. My advice to someone going through a loss is to not wait but to try and process the loss while it is fresh. The pain is so intense no one wants to face it. But...it will not go away. So, as difficult as doing so might be, the best thing to ensure your healing is to feel the pain and work through it so healing can begin.

I saw this delay of healing in my own family. My mom was the prime example of how unprocessed grief can cause years and even a lifetime of pain and possibly turn into physical and mental illness.

I also experienced it firsthand by not processing the early loss of my dad when he left me at age three, followed by the loss of my mom as she slipped into a deep depression.

I started smoking cigarettes at ten and continued for a decade, thankfully quitting the habit by the time I turned twenty. I also smoked marijuana to numb my mind, something I really can't believe now. I hate the feeling of being high, always have, but I still did it starting at a very young age. I was desperate to stay numb. Then, after Jimmy's death, at age seventeen, I moved away and never really faced the pain. I suffered from low self-esteem, anxiety, and an eating disorder, never feeling like I was worthy of a good life. All I could do was survive.

It took the loss of Jack for me to actually feel deep pain so big I couldn't numb it forever. I had to learn to manage it. Thankfully, I turned to exercise first.

Unfortunately, I didn't have the support of my husband with this coping mechanism. While I turned to physical activity, Bill turned to less healthy distractions, and that was hard on me. I needed a partner to get through this hell but felt alone in this journey. Even though I felt alone, I still pushed through the inertia.

You, too, can do this.

If you don't consciously choose how to manage grief, it's easy to slip into habits like abusing alcohol or medication, turning to pornography, seeking relief in sexual indulgence, overspending, or becoming addicted to gambling—among other escapes.. The Grief Recovery Method handbook calls these behaviors STERBs, or short term energy relieving behaviors. Don't judge yourself; these behaviors are natural responses to pain. But remember, they are distractions, not solutions, and they only delay the healing process. It's important to recognize when these patterns become unhealthy and start making changes. Self-medicating needs to be addressed for true healing to begin.

I also indulged in unhealthy behaviors at first, but when I saw Bill lose himself in his grief, I vowed to choose something different. I turned to the sea. I took to walking by the ocean as a way to calm myself and reflect on my loss. I was lucky to have healing water so close and had gotten into the habit of walking the three blocks to the Pacific Ocean every day. Before Jack died, I used to run on the bike path at the edge of the sand. I loved the view of the beach from its border, where I could watch the water darken the sand with each wave and the cotton candy clouds hang over the sunset in the distance. But after Jack's death, the bike path wasn't enough. I didn't want to take in the beach like a work of art. I had to be in it. I walked along the edge of the water, letting the calming waves and sea-salt smell surround me. The ocean brought solace.

On that first walk, I went all the way to the Huntington Beach Pier and back, seventeen city blocks each way. I couldn't believe it took thirty years and a tragic loss to get me to do that. It became my daily walk for the next year. The thundering waves howled with me as I sobbed, and the sea-salt spray mingled with my tears. The ocean grieved with me every day that year.

Sometimes I spoke to Jack at the seaside, sometimes I just talked to myself. I started collecting shells. I learned later that many people associate seashells with grief. The empty shell is reminiscent of a body left behind after the soul departs. I didn't know that at the time, but something drew me to them. Some days, I would ask Jack to help me look for these treasures, and each special find became a reminder of his presence in the world. I still have many of those shells in a vase in my home. They are one of my most special possessions.

In my search for seashells, I also began collecting sea glass. I found it to be a very special and even magical find in my beach searches. I met a woman at church who invited me on a sea glass hunt south of Huntington. She had visited this beach many times over the years, after an almost fatal accident left her brain-damaged. Collecting sea glass was part of her recovery. It gave her purpose, a small goal to work toward. It helped her practice restoring her motor skills and brought beauty to her home. I, with my grief-stricken brain and crisis-fatigued body, understood. We shared stories of our losses as we walked. After that day, I returned many times (and still do!) to continue my own healing by hunting for sea glass. I find that I, too, have been broken and dashed upon the waves, polished with salt, and refined by the experience.

Dragonflies are another symbol that offered me that glimmer of hope every time I saw one. They showed up regularly in my initial grieving period, starting in my mother's yard the day after Jack's funeral. To me, they always felt like Jack. They continue to surround me and hold special meaning to this day—from my passing by a single dragonfly on a walk to a large cloud of red dragonflies in a lagoon at Jack's second-year remembrance. In almost every part of the world, the dragonfly symbolizes change, transformation, adaptability, and self-realization. Because of this, many people see dragonflies as a sign of a loved one who has passed on from this earth.

Seashells, sea glass, and dragonflies became important symbols to me after Jack's death. I saw them as messages from him, and finding them reassured me of his presence. He had held such a huge space in my life that my mind wasn't ready to accept the finality of his death. I still needed to search for a connection to him. I've read that this type of collecting is common after loss—it reminds us of the loved one's presence even when they are not physically there, like a blanket or doll reminds a toddler of its mother.

What reminds you of your loved one? Are they sending any special messages your way? Many people begin seeing dragonflies, birds, seashells, heart-shaped rocks, or special clouds when they start looking for reminders of the person they lost. These tiny treasures can help you form a positive relationship with your memories and feel your loved one is with you. Start a collection! Let yourself feel a small surge of happiness when you find something special. Let it give you hope.

What gives you that glimmer of hope, of healing, of well-being, and what can you do to fan that spark and help it grow? A glimmer can turn into a bright light that leads the way.

As I write this, I have just returned from collecting shells. Many families were at the beach on this sunny Saturday. Young people lounged or ran around in groups having fun. I felt a twinge of sad remembrance of times with my kids when they were little, warning them to not go too far away as they looked for shells and built sandcastles.

Today a young boy came up to me as a tear ran down my cheek. He had his hand held out with a little clam shell shaped like a tiny butterfly.

He said, "Here, this is for you."

I looked up and smiled. "Thank you, Jack."

Now, I'm going to contradict myself a bit. Healing from loss is such a personal journey, and I can share only what worked for me, but I found that my collections of Jack memorabilia helped tremendously…to a point. However, after a time and as tough as it was, I found it necessary to let go of some things. I couldn't live surrounded by vestiges of Jack's ghost. At first, I wanted to keep everything, but over time the vastness of the collection became overwhelming. I had to learn to be discerning in what shells and feathers I brought home.

The process of letting go of objects that remind us of our loved one is very personal and will be different for each person. I found what works for me: a curio cabinet in my front room that contains pictures of Jack, the most special shells and feathers I have collected since his passing, and other memorabilia that I like to look at to remind me of him. I kept his water polo backpack and Bill kept his wallet, the two things he carried on him every day.

I also have a guest room closet full of his clothing and boxes with his belongings. I know I can't keep these things forever. I have already done two purges, and I want to decrease further. But I don't beat myself up about not rushing to finish the job.

Since this is a difficult process, give yourself permission to take as much time as you need. I suggest you also take this in stages.

Here's an idea. Give yourself a goal of looking through one box. Then go through the box and decide what you can let go of and keep meaningful items or ones you can't decide on. It's okay to not know yet; you can decide later. But make a date for yourself to get started.

The goal I set for myself was to have one or two storage bins, like the boxes I keep my Christmas decorations in, that contained only the most special items I chose to keep. I currently have five boxes, plus all the clothing I mentioned, so I have a few dates to place on my own calendar to continue the process. I feel that after finishing this book I will be ready to do the next reduction of Jack's belongings. I will make a second donation to Robyne's Nest or another charity of my choice. And, of course, I will always stay open to receiving the little gifts that Jack leaves for me on our walks together.

As the seasons changed, at least as much as they do in Southern California, I changed. I began to see the variations in nature as a beautiful pattern I wasn't meant to understand. On my walks at the shore, some days there were no shells, and some days there was an abundance. Some things just are and I was learning to accept that.

Another way I started healing was to practice saying yes again. I had been hiding in my grief, and going out into the world was a gargantuan task. I started small—saying yes to a run in the hills with the mom of one of Jack's best friends, saying yes to coffee with a friend and confiding in her about all the secret struggles that come with grief. In these small ways, I let myself say yes to being in the world again. Over time, I got braver. My first big yes was to an invite from a fellow water polo mom to a beach yoga group. My own yes shocked me on its way out of my mouth. But I was practicing. I had to try on that yes to find the person I wanted to be after Jack. That beach yoga community welcomed me with open arms, and they have been one of the touchstones that has kept me going since.

In the first year after losing Jack, I was invited to two weddings, and I said yes to both. The first was for my niece, a beautiful celebration at an old Catholic church in Los Angeles. I thought that if I decided to go, I would have to compartmentalize my emotions. I didn't want my sadness to ruin the celebration for everyone else. But I found that burying my sadness was impossible. And guess what? I couldn't help bringing my grief with me, but I was still happy for my niece. I was able to feel both joy and sadness at the same time. I celebrated the joy of a new relationship bond in a sacred wedding ceremony, being filled with love for the new couple while also feeling sad that Jack was never going to experience this. I could hold both. I am so grateful for that lesson.

The second wedding was for some good friends and took place in Redlands at an orange grove. The smell of orange blossoms filled the warm Southern California air, and the feeling of excitement radiated among the wedding party and guests. It truly felt like a fairytale, and I was happy to be there to celebrate. I was able to take my lesson from that first wedding and actually look forward to the second. I knew I could handle being there, because I understood I didn't have to ignore my heart. My wish for you, dear reader, is that you will say yes to invitations, get dressed up, and set your mind to the idea that you will have fun! Although the event may also have moments of sadness, you will be able to ride the wave of grief and still celebrate. What a gift.

I embraced every invitation and just said yes to all of them. Now, looking back, I realize how much courage that took. When you go through a major loss, the first instinct is to hide away so no one has to see the ugly crying, the pained look on your face. It takes courage to say yes, but this, my friend, is how you move forward in healing. Through every yes, I began to see the shape of a new life.

Can you see a glimmer of healing on the horizon? Now that you feel hope and you have tapped that glimmer of light as you move out of shock, you are ready to begin this climb in earnest. You have walked through the valley and turned your gaze upward. You are ready to work toward healing. It's time to move into grief work. And that's where we're going in Chapter Six.

You can do it. I've paved the way and I will show you how.

Okay, I Need Therapy

So many things—sometimes it feels like everything—remind me of Jack. Going out meant constant reminders that hurled me into spirals of memories. There were times that I thought I would lose my mind or die myself because I couldn't escape the torment in my own head. Saying yes to life was an important first step, but it wasn't enough.

I started to go out of the house for everyday tasks. Over time, the visiting slowed. People started checking in once a week, then only on special days. I couldn't rely on thoughtful care packages anymore. I tossed the flowers, and replacements stopped arriving. The meal train ended, I returned to the grocery store, and life continued. These errands were often the hardest outings for me. The familiarity was a reminder of life with Jack, a life I could never have again.

Grocery shopping was grueling. I was suddenly shopping for three instead of four, no longer buying food to sustain Jack's athletic build, which had been at the center of our grocery lists. There was an invisible hole in our lists now, an unspoken sadness for everything I wasn't buying. It was particularly hard at Trader Joe's, where my family had happy memories. My kids and I had spent many afternoons looking for the hidden bunny or turtle to get a lollipop and asking for stickers at the checkout. I had built a rapport with the employees. Now, seeing so many of Jack's favorite foods made me feel so alone in my grief. I was grateful for the mask mandate that kept my grief private.

On my very first Trader Joe's run, just weeks after Jack's death, the woman in front of me in the checkout line was struggling to manage her energetic son, and I felt like I was watching a scene of me and seven-year-old Jack. He was jumping around, couldn't stand still, his mop of sun-bleached blonde hair flopping with each hop, asking for a fruit stick (Jack's favorite) from the checkout kiosk. I had to turn to the side to not completely break down and look like a lunatic staring at a stranger. I actually pinched my hand between my thumb and index finger to calm myself, took some deep breaths, and closed my eyes until they left.

As I stepped up to the cashier, I recognized a familiar face. It was one of my favorite TJ employees, a young man who always engaged me in conversation and asked about my family. He saw me there many times with my kids.

He asked the usual, "How are you today?"

Unbelievably, I found myself saying, "Not so good. My son died by suicide a few weeks ago."

The young man looked startled, the smile melted off his face as he came around the counter and broke protocol by giving me a big, much-needed hug. He then said, "Wait here, I'll be right back," and returned with three giant bouquets of flowers "on the house." He walked me to the door with concern in his eyes. Since then, the Trader Joe's employees always give me an extra hug. They still ask how I'm doing every time I shop there. This made a seemingly impossible task, shopping after the loss of my son, into such a comforting experience. Although the outing was still difficult, each time it became less and less painful.

Today I can actually look forward to shopping. I no longer have tears and a sad heart. I do sometimes pause over the Orange Chicken, one of Jack's favorites, and feel a twinge of sad remembrance, but it's always dwarfed by the happy memory of how much he loved it.

You may need more time before you go back to your favorite spots. That's okay! Give yourself permission to visit stores, eat at restaurants, and go on outings that carry no memories for you. Then, when you're ready, you can reintroduce your familiar locations.

The crazy thing about healing is it is so unpredictable. Some days going out on my own was fine. Some days they were not. Sometimes outings with friends and family went smoothly; other times I was hit by a tsunami of grief and had to leave early. I just never knew what would trigger me and send me spiraling again.

My true healing started when I realized and accepted that my walks, exercises, and outings weren't cutting it on their own. I didn't need to be the one who knew how to heal myself. There were wonderful people out there who did. I needed professional help, not just for me but for the sake of my family. But how? Who? I didn't know where to start.

Then I realized, I didn't need to know. I just picked up the phone and called the number on the back of my insurance card. They connected me to a therapist. Can you believe it was that easy? What a Godsend!

My therapist and I started meeting weekly, and she recommended several books about how the body is affected by unresolved grief and trauma. I read three influential books: *The Body Keeps the Score* by Bessel Van Der Klok, M.D., a book about healing the brain and body after psychological trauma; *When the Body Says NO* by Gabor Mate, M.D., which explores the stress-disease connection; and *Getting Past Your Past* by Francine Shapiro, Ph.D., which advocates for self-help techniques from EMDR therapy. These books helped me understand the mind-body connection and how unresolved grief can lead to disease. They inspired me—I was now on a mission to find ways to support my brain *and* my body through my grief recovery.

My therapist began weekly EMDR sessions. EMDR, or eye movement, desensitization, and reprocessing, is a very simple but effective treatment that stimulates several senses while you access painful memories in order to manage your brain's emotional response to them. My therapist used a screen with a glowing green ball that moved back and forth like a game of Pong. I laughed the first time I saw it—how funny that a low-tech device that looked like an old video game could produce such profound results. I was instructed to follow the ball with my eyes while I held an electrode in each hand. Each time the ball bounced off the edge of the screen, the electrodes would buzz and a sound would play. I was getting simultaneous full sensory stimuli: visual from the ball moving, physical from the eye movement, auditory from the sound emitted, and tactile from the electrode buzz.

Then came the hard part. My therapist would guide me as I thought about a particular trauma. Something about the sensory overwhelm made me particularly vulnerable as I relived my worst memories, especially the moment I got the voicemail about Jack.

This memory would surface often in my daily life, and it almost always led to a panic attack. I would get short of breath, start sweating, and feel sick to my stomach. I was having trouble sleeping, especially when I had to sleep in the day after a night shift. The first time I described this memory during EMDR, it felt as fresh as the day it happened. I cried and cried, all of my panic symptoms rushing in at the very painful memory.

Then, like a miracle, the process started working.

After describing that horrible memory several times, I started experiencing fewer of the troubling physical sensations that accompanied the memory. Eventually, I was able to think about that event without feeling panic at all. I could finally sleep again. It was still a traumatic memory, but I could remember it without being overwhelmed. This transformation truly amazed me. I am incredibly grateful for this type of therapy and believe it may help you too.

Over time, we began expanding to memories outside of my life with Jack. We realized that Jack's death was just a piece of my grief puzzle—I had childhood traumas to process as well. My therapist worked through these memories with me and helped me unhook them from the panic and overwhelm they used to bring up. EMDR was the turning-point tool for me. I was finally starting to really heal.

I also fell in love with sound baths—environments in which a person is completely immersed in curated sounds that put the brain into a meditative state. The deep relaxation is so healing. Sound healing works by using specific sound frequencies to stimulate the body's natural healing mechanisms. When we are exposed to certain sounds, like those emitted by singing bowls or special instruments, our brain waves synchronize to the frequency of the sound, which can promote relaxation, reduce stress and anxiety, and promote physical healing. Sound healing can offer a range of benefits, including stress reduction, improved sleep, pain relief, enhanced creativity and intuition, and greater emotional balance and well-being. It can also be helpful for those experiencing depression, anxiety, or PTSD.

In addition to private therapy, sound baths, and EMDR, my therapist also recommended group therapy. Bill found a support group for people experiencing loss: Grief Share. There are Grief Share communities all over the country. He wanted to be around others experiencing similar emotional wreckage. It can be comforting to share your experience with others who understand. I agreed to go.

Bill and I found our local Grief Share space set up in a large room full of round tables. A box of tissues sat in the middle of each one—the classic grief centerpiece. The room quickly filled with people of different ages and backgrounds. The session worked like this: First a video was shown about various ways in which grief touches our lives. The program spanned thirteen weeks, with a different video shown each week. The series was shown on a continuous loop, so people could jump in anytime and continue for as long as they wanted. A handbook accompanied each lesson with homework to prepare prior to the class, but people could move at their own pace, no pressure. The lessons were short, and the videos showed real people sharing different aspects of their experience with loss.

Sounds great, right?

When that first video started, I had to put every ounce of my concentration on not busting out laughing. The production was so outdated, the clothes must have been from the eighties, and the people sharing had such deadpan deliveries…I honestly felt like I was watching an oldie-but-goodie *Saturday Night Live* skit. I looked around the room—surely everyone else was holding in their laughter too. The video was hilarious! No… just me? Somehow my secret laughter felt good. I had my own private little joke, one that distracted me from my pain and allowed me to embrace the absurdity of grief.

After the video finished, we were encouraged to talk to others at our table and share our stories. Bill opened up about our loss in a very emotional way. I think it was good for him to talk out loud about losing Jack. I was not able to say anything; how did I follow that outpouring of emotion? After the session finished, two other families came up to us and said that they had each also lost a nineteen-year-old son. It was nice to connect with families who understood.

Bill and I went back a few times. Having a bit of community definitely helped us take those early steps toward healing. But the groups changed each week, and we never really made connections. Overall, Grief Share was not the right therapy for me. I needed something different.

Three months after Jack died, I reached out to the mortuary where Jack had been laid to rest. They have an in-house grief counselor, Anne-Marie Lockmyer, who came very highly recommended. I had turned down the service when it was offered by the mortuary director at the time of the funeral, but I was now ready to try anything, so I left a message on her voicemail. When Anne-Marie called me back, I told her about Jack through tears and sobs. She said that although my loss was so traumatic and still so fresh, my asking for support was a good sign, and it might be time to start a healing program. If I wanted to, I could join the next session of the Grief Recovery Method (GRM).

What did I have to lose? I wanted to do anything, everything I could to heal. I could just try it out, right? I asked for the class info, and she gave me the Zoom link and schedule. I didn't know what to expect; I just jumped in with blind faith. Boy, was that faith rewarded.

The Grief Recovery Method was exactly what I needed. I had sequential, progressive lessons to look forward to and a systematic series of homework to follow. Anne-Marie and her specialist partner and husband Ron Gray started the first session with an invitation to share our stories. There were six of us in the group, and we became a little grief family. I told the condensed version of Jack's story that had become so practiced.

"I lost my son to suicide four and a half months ago. He was nineteen years old, a college student on a water polo scholarship. He was a sweet soul who loved his friends and family. Jack was a COVID casualty in a way, even though he never contracted the virus. The isolation of the pandemic stole his sport and independence, which contributed to his having a psychiatric meltdown that ended in his unfortunate death."

I pushed through the giant lump in my throat and tears stinging my eyes to say this. My newly formed family cried with me. We took a break from the Zoom for everyone to recover. Something about a perfect, beautiful, athletic, sweet young man who had everything going for him ending his life is just so difficult to fathom.

A circle of trust was formed, the deep dark stories waiting to be shared. There is something special about the comfort of hearing someone else's sadness when you are experiencing something similar. Even if the losses are different, the pain of the loss is universal and needs to be shared with another human. This was the premise of Grief Share, but I found that sharing to a different room every week wasn't enough for me. It took a structured format of sharing with a trusted circle. And we didn't just share the base story. We shared the unsaid emotions, the things we wish we had communicated to our lost loved one.

That's a pillar of the Grief Recovery Method: The brain thinks of all the unsaid messages to the loved one, then spirals into regret for all that was left unsaid. The Grief Recovery Method offers a formula for building trust in your group and sharing all these unspoken messages with them. The lost loved one does not have to receive the message for it to be a powerful tool to relieve your mind of regret—just sharing the message in a trusted and supportive community can start to heal your broken heart.

The Grief Recovery Method is such an effective way to process grief. I went into the program thinking I would be dealing only with the loss of Jack, just those fresh wounds that wouldn't close. But I soon realized that I was opening decades of unresolved pain. And I wasn't sure if I was ready to go that deep. I had no idea what I was getting into. But that program was exactly where I needed to be.

Where do you need to be to heal? Only you can answer, and only after you get out there and try different approaches. Private therapy with EMDR and the Grief Recovery Method group were the answers for me. Find your own corner of the grief recovery world. Move in and let yourself sigh with relief. You are home. You are safe. In this environment, you can do the work.

Let's keep scaling this mountain together. In the next chapter, I'll share how this mad dash toward healing the scars Jack left grew into a healing for all my broken parts—even childhood wounds.

CHAPTER SEVEN

Loss and I Are Old Friends

Jack was not the first person I'd lost too young. By the time of Jack's death, loss and I were old friends.

Loss first visited me at the tender age of three. Then five. Then ten. Then seventeen.

The Grief Recovery Method requires participants to write out a grief timeline. According to the method's framework, there are over forty distinct types of loss that elicit grief. Big or small, they all matter. When I did my grief timeline, I started with the big three: my biological dad's leaving and death, my brother Jimmy's death, and Jack's death. But the Grief Recovery curriculum helped me realize that I had many more.

Major loss had paid me many other visits that left scars. I was trying to heal from Jack's death, but it was only one of the open wounds. I had pushed the others down and tried to forget about them, as most of us are taught to do. Time had eased the stings enough that I could keep living, but the wounds were still there. Still open, still bleeding. Time hadn't healed them on its own. *I* needed to do it.

The Grief Recovery Method describes past losses as heavy stones in a backpack. I had carried the first six stones for a long time. They were heavy, and they required energy to lug them through life. But I had gotten used to their weight on my back so they didn't hurt. Still, damn, was I tired. Then Jack died, and an incomprehensibly huge boulder was thrown onto the pile. This stone was too heavy to lift. I couldn't move through life with it—I had to let that boulder go to survive. I started therapy and then found my Grief Recovery Method group to get out from under that boulder.

We all carry baggage. You, too, lug your backpack of stones through your life, straining a little more than you would without them. If you've experienced traumatic loss like me, you know how it feels to be crushed under the weight of a boulder, to pull on a backpack too heavy to lift. You need to empty your backpack of that boulder! But why would you stop there? Why remove only one?

Jack's death was my biggest boulder, but I didn't want to do all the work of removing it just to be left with the same heavy backpack. If I could take Jack's boulder out of the backpack, I could remove the rest. I knew this was my opportunity, what I had been waiting for my whole adult life. I was going to empty that damn backpack.

Loss first visited me when my biological father left our family. I was three years old, and feeling him try to pull my brother and me away from our mother is my very first memory. I don't remember him outside of that one glimpse. I know his name was James Laurence Zimmerman, but everyone called

A Thousand Little Memories

him "Jim Zim." Even if I don't remember him, I grieved for him. Working through Jack's death with the Grief Recovery Method helped me see that even this early memory was a loss I had grieved over. I grew up with an underlying anxiety and fear of abandonment. My father died when I was fourteen, without ever seeing me again. I mourned the dad I never knew.

Next I lost my innocence. My mom remarried, and her new husband adopted my brother and me. He then proceeded to abuse us for fifteen years. I lost the innocent outlook a child has before they've been truly hurt. The Grief Recovery Method gave me the tools to process the pain from the abuse, so that I could let it go and not continue to hurt myself with the memories.

The next loss was another one I hadn't realized I was still mourning. I felt like I lost my youth at fifteen when I became pregnant with my son, Joshua. That time in my life, which should have been carefree, was instead filled with responsibility. Even though becoming a mom at sixteen was not ideal, it actually turned my life around. I was a party girl before I became pregnant and a straight A student the year after. I became self-reliant. I had no choice; I loved my son so much that simply caring for him made me a better, more responsible person. Still, there was some sadness there about what else could have been.

The next loss was the big one—the only loss I was truly aware of before I started my Grief Recovery timeline. When I was seventeen, my brother Jimmy, my best friend and only confidant through all the shared pain and love of our childhood, died. He was only nineteen, the same age as Jack. It was one week before my high school graduation. I never processed

Jimmy's death—it was too difficult, I was too young, and I had no model for healthy grief. Our mother had no support and was so distraught that all I could think of to save myself was to leave. I had a son to provide for and so much pain to escape. Josh's dad and I moved to North Carolina a month later. I trained myself to stop thinking about Jimmy.

The next thing I lost was my first love. Josh's dad was my first boyfriend, and we had been together since I was a fourteen-year-old freshman at our tiny Catholic school. He was a Detroit City bad boy with gentle brown eyes who wore a cowboy hat over his long auburn hair. I think I liked that my parents disapproved of him. We had so much fun together. We had a precious son. I thought this was true love, but we were so young, and I never had a healthy relationship modeled for me.

After Josh was born, I held most of the responsibility, and the relationship changed. Josh's dad was never the partner or father I wanted him to be. In North Carolina, I played house for a year until I realized the relationship was not going anywhere. We split when Josh was three, and I moved back home to Michigan. When Josh was four, he was severely injured while under his father's care. I stopped talking to him for many years after that. It was a slow loss: a piece-by-piece breakdown of the man I thought he could be. I never processed that loss either. I had to think of Joshua's best interest, and I had to keep blindly marching along the path of survival.

Shortly after I moved back to Michigan, I met James's dad at the steakhouse where I had a waitressing job. He was charming, gave me lots of attention, and he reminded me so much of my brother Jimmy. My grieving heart was comforted. And he offered me a way out of living back home with my mother. What a plus!

So on I went to a new relationship. And even when I started to see the drinking problem peeking out from behind all the charisma and good times, I viewed him as my ticket out. I followed him to California. We had James shortly after, and his drinking problem got worse. He became violent and abusive. Another relationship ended poorly, another love lost. Again, I never really grieved this loss, just moved it aside so I could continue surviving. I had two boys to protect now.

Then, loss left me alone for a while. I met Bill, my knight in shining armor, who loved me despite my baggage—two sons from two failed relationships. Suddenly, I didn't have to do it all alone anymore! We dated for seven years, finally getting married after I completed nursing school and started working as an RN. With Bill, our new little family experienced joys I could never afford before. As my two older boys grew up and left the nest, I faced the bittersweet loss of watching them go. Then came Jack, followed by Tori, and we had some truly good years. We lived in Huntington Beach, and then, due to circumstances I didn't fully understand at the time, we moved to Napa for ten years before eventually finding our way back to my beloved Huntington.

Then the big boulder fell. Jack's suicide was the loss to end all losses, the moment that will forever be my "before and after" moment. This was the loss I came here to process—the boulder I came to unpack.

In the next few Grief Recovery sessions, I started voicing what I most regretted, wished were different, and was thankful for in my entire relationship with Jack. I gushed about it all—from the moment I found out I was pregnant on a sunny, early spring Saturday, to the last time I talked to Jack and told him I loved him. Over time, I began to shift my perspective on Jack's life. Instead of focusing on all the unlived moments Jack should have had, I felt immense gratitude for his incredible nineteen years of life. This became a technique, something I could consciously do when the sadness was overwhelming. I learned how to choose to focus my thoughts on gratitude, and that gratitude became real.

In doing this work, the process was to make a timeline of all my losses, then another timeline of one loss, a "relationship graph," and share that with our little grief family. By doing so, the constant guilt and regret were replaced with peace.

Now let me tell you, I still have my sad days. Sometimes the feelings of deep sadness and loss overwhelm me, and all I can do is cry. I still mourn the awesome adventurous life that I know Jack would have had past nineteen. I miss his physical presence and grieve for the unlived moments we could have had together. But those sad days come and go, and I'm still here. I can always find something about Jack to be thankful for. I harbor no guilt or regrets, because I left nothing unspoken between us. I shared every thought I have ever had about Jack with my Grief Recovery family, and I know that Jack heard it all. He knows exactly how much I have loved him through every moment of his life and beyond. There is nothing left to say. I can leave that boulder behind.

Suddenly my backpack was a little lighter. Then a little lighter still. Other stones were falling out! I learned so much about loss and grief from unpacking Jack's boulder. I could look back at each loss and see it for what it was: a moment of permanent silence when I had more to say. I could see my not-so-helpful survival patterns and coping mechanisms solidifying with each story. There was "past me," running from the emotions, putting others first, and ignoring the impulse to vent my frustrations. Jack's death actually opened my eyes to the unfulfilling life I had created for myself in my attempts to run away from loss. Now I could finally take the time to say what needed to be said. The new me was embracing these emotions and taking care of myself first.

Over the next few months, I removed just about every damn stone in that bag. I said everything I wished I'd said to my sons' fathers, to my horrible stepfather, to my absent dad. Even to Jimmy. Just like I did with Jack, I looked at the complete picture of their presence in my life, and I finally allowed myself the space to share it all with my GRM group. And with all the repressed feelings went the stones. Stone by stone, my backpack got lighter.

If you constantly relive the events of a loved one's death, combing through every detail looking for more weight to add to your boulder of regret, then give the Grief Recovery Method a try. There are groups throughout the country and even more online. Good luck in this endeavor, I know these losses can be tough to think about and can be uncomfortable to tackle the long-hidden grief from past loss and also difficult to want to process a current loss, but I can say you will be so much better in the long run if you put in the effort now. You have the reason and the energy for this healing—just do it!

Leaving those stones behind inspired me to also stop dragging along all the coping mechanisms with me. As you can see, I have a complicated life story. Layers of loss and trauma formed a suit of armor I proudly wore, convinced I was a pro at this grief thing. How wrong I was.

That armor was really a messy haze of unhealthy thoughts and behavior patterns that I was hiding behind. They kept me running on the hamster wheel of daily life, but they were preventing me from processing the grief that had accumulated through the decades. In short, I was faking it—not only fooling others but myself along the way. That was how my family had dealt with tragedy in my childhood. I learned to ignore, to be silent, to move on. I didn't have a model of a healthy grief processing, so I lived in fear of more loss. I clung to good things that came along without realizing why. I would keep my head down, keep my sorrow bottled up, keep the peace at all costs. This was the "stellar soldier" I thought I was proud to be, the woman who could take calls from Jack's doctors and tell my family everything was going to be okay, who could stifle her pain to buy others another minute of hope. I thought I was resilient, but I was just hanging on.

I clung tightly to the vision of a "normal" family, something I never had growing up. My childhood was far from ordinary: I lost my father at a young age, was raised by an unfit stepfather, became a teen mom during my junior year of high school, and lost my once-inseparable brother just a week before graduation. I had no idea what a "normal" family looked like, so I invented one in my mind. This fantasy became my guiding light, leading me through life without taking responsibility or making informed choices. I ran away with the first boy who showed me attention and clung to him long after I knew he wasn't right for me. When that relationship failed, I latched onto the next one, desperate for the love and stability I had imagined in my head. I even moved to another state in pursuit of that dream.

When that relationship fell apart, I still couldn't shake the image of the perfect little family. I didn't realize then that my desperation for this ideal came from grief and a deep fear of further loss. Then I met Bill, a strong, independent man who knew how to achieve big things. Our personalities seemed to complement each other perfectly. I thought I finally had the family I'd dreamed of all my life.

But achieving that dream only intensified my desperation. Now that I had the family I wanted, I was determined never to let it go. I sacrificed my own desires and needs to maintain the peace and preserve the dream. I worked part-time as a nurse to supplement Bill's income, took care of the house and kids, and did everything to keep the family together. I never asked for more, too afraid to risk what I thought was a good thing.

Although I wasn't completely unhappy, I wasn't getting my needs met or feeling like we had a true partnership. I blamed the stress of raising kids and keeping the household running. I wasn't thinking about my own happiness or aware of the root of the problem, so I kept the marriage going. When Bill lost his job, and we had to sell our dream home, I became a full-time night-shift nurse. On top of all the "mom" responsibilities, I now had to be the emotional support for a husband who was struggling to get back on his feet.

When Jack moved back home after his dorms closed during Covid, our seemingly perfect family found itself stuck together for six months, with no clear end to the lockdown in sight. The pressure of that time brought all our hidden imperfections to the surface. I was overwhelmed and on the verge of imploding, yet I never asked for anything. I was holding on too tightly to the image of our perfect family to risk a confrontation. Deep down, I knew something was fundamentally wrong with the marriage, but I couldn't pinpoint what it was. I assumed it was just the stress of raising a family and believed things would eventually get better. My past losses had turned me into such a people-pleaser that I would sacrifice my own sanity just to keep the peace.

With the loss of Jack, my world cracked wide open. I no longer felt the pressure to continue the illusion of the perfect family, because now it was gone forever, never to return. I just couldn't continue the facade. Even after Bill found a job, the pattern of unhappiness in our marriage continued. The Grief Recovery Method also helped me recognize this pattern and let it go. I didn't have to sacrifice my sanity for the illusion of the perfect family anymore.

My other main coping mechanism was codependency. I dealt with grief by ignoring it in favor of helping others. I couldn't take the time to fully feel Jimmy's death or the end of relationships when I had children who depended on me. Over the years, this grew into a codependent helper complex. I felt valued only when I was needed. I'm sure you can see echoes of this in my self-sacrifice for the image of our perfect family. In reality, my marriage with Bill had functioned only because of this need to be needed. My urge to sacrifice worked perfectly for Bill—he always got his way and we never argued. If there was a disagreement, I felt the battle wasn't worth fighting most of the time. Plus, avoiding the fight and making us work was a task that gave me validation. And Bill always gave me that validation. His constant gratitude for how I held the family together fed my codependent ego. I was the *only* one holding us together.

I take full responsibility for this pattern. A mash-up of codependent habits that I had developed over a lifetime of suppressing and ignoring my own inner world. Codependency was my comfort zone.

In Grief Recovery, I learned to recognize this pattern. Unpacking my backpack opened my eyes to the unhappy, unspoken life I was leading. And I couldn't go back. I had to take care of myself instead of Bill for a bit. Eventually, I had to be honest with myself. I had to say the unspoken: The best way for me to take care of myself was to do it without Bill. We needed our own healing spaces, and I needed peace. I told him I was moving out.

Bill wasn't equipped to handle the news, and within a week, he had a mini-crisis. I was so tempted to slip back into my old role as the helper and try to save him, but I held my ground. I realized that I could take care only of myself—I had no control over how someone else chose to respond or not respond. It may sound harsh, but this was the moment when I had to put myself first. I still held hope that one day we would both be at similar points in our healing journeys, allowing us to live the happily ever after we once dreamed of.

Although I made the difficult decision to separate from my husband, I don't in any way advocate for someone else to do this. I continue to be a strong believer of the sanctity of marriage, and my intention in living separately was to create space to heal as individuals, so we could come back together in a stronger union. A part of me still holds that hope.

Friend, you can see just how much baggage healing with the Grief Recovery Method helped me leave behind. The same freedom is possible for you. You can unburden yourself from the pain of a lifetime of loss, and you can let go of the lies you told yourself to hide from that pain. You can even shift your perspective on your worst day. Maybe the death that broke you also broke down everything holding you back. It's time to empty your backpack and take your first unhindered step.

What does that life look like for you?

Mine looked like this: Here I was, living in a cute little three-bedroom apartment, three blocks from the beach where I did yoga. Tori lived with me, but some days I was alone. I left my fractured marriage behind in the hopes of reuniting with a healed Bill in the future. I emptied my backpack and took off my armor. I let go of my desperate need for the perfect family and my codependent habit of putting others first. I reached a place of peace about Jack's death, and that peace spread to all the corners of my tired soul. I let it all go.

Jack's death and the pilgrimage it put me on had blown up every piece of my life, every piece of me. I was nothing. Just a woman walking on the beach.

I was free.

And in that nothing, I started to wonder who I really was, and who I wanted to be. I had crested the Mountain of Hope and began to look toward the next peak. I lifted my face toward the Mountain of Recreation. When you're ready, join me.

PART 3:
THE MOUNTAIN
OF RECREATION

The Phoenix Rising

CHAPTER EIGHT

An Uncommon Path

Alone, all alone, and yet strangely happy. As I walked the beach from my new apartment, I looked out at the ocean and saw a future as vast as the open sea. This was the first time in a very long time that I was living on my own. Well, sort of— my daughter Tori still lived with me and I was so grateful for that, but I was solo in the sense that I didn't have a partner. I had decided to separate from Bill. Even though I was alone, I felt a newfound freedom that was liberating. My apartment was several blocks from the family rental home and a short six blocks to the pier. I felt a new connection to this little beachside community and felt like I was moving into a brand-new start for myself.

Who was I now? I had always been defined by outside forces—a daughter, a sister, a girlfriend, a mother too soon, a nurse, a wife. And now, I was just me. I liked it but also felt insecure and unsure of my future.

After all the therapy, especially the Grief Recovery Method, I was in a state of what my life coach Lisa J. calls "zero-point energy." It's the limitless potential that can only exist when everything you knew has been stripped away. As Lisa J. says, when you have nothing, you have everything. (I'll get to how I found Lisa J. later in Chapter Nine.)

When Bill lost his job, we also lost our financial stability, and in a lot of ways, I lost my sanity. I became the sole breadwinner, working all night shifts, while continuing to be the caretaker of the family and carrying the new weight of financial uncertainty. The dream home we had put so much money and effort into perfecting was gone. Jack was gone. My marriage as I once knew it was gone. And a big part of myself was gone.

Looking back, I see that it wasn't my sanity I lost—it was the illusion that my life was okay. That *I* was okay. As I shared in the last chapter, I learned through my Grief Recovery journey that the pain from past losses was dictating my decisions in an unhealthy way.

I was stripped down to nothing. But in this stripped-down state, anything was possible. I could have closed myself in a cave of self-pity for all that I had gone through in such a short amount of time, but instead I made the conscious decision to break out of that cave and fill my life with whatever would make this new me happy. I just had to find what that was.

I hired Lisa J. when I didn't even entirely know what a "life coach" was. What I did know was that I needed direction to get where I wanted to go. Honestly, I needed direction to even decide *where* I wanted to go. When you experience losing your identity due to a major loss—such as losing a child, a spouse, a career job, a marriage, your health, your normalcy—you have the chance to change. To recreate yourself. I hope that you, too, will come to see loss as an opportunity rather than an end. You may have lost everything, but you can use that zero-point energy to create a new reality, something even better than the world the loss took from you. I know this to my core, and it is my intention to help you tap into this power in this chapter.

My life was now a void that I could fill with things that made me feel good. I had gained thirty pounds and watched hundreds of hours of Netflix in the year after Jack died, and while I didn't judge myself for using food, alcohol, and TV to distract from my initial shock, these things made my body feel bloated and my mind sluggish. I was still doing my daily beach walk and the occasional yoga class, but it wasn't enough exercise to keep me feeling healthy. I needed to move more to feel good. I started doing day hikes in Crystal Cove State Park or at the beaches in Huntington and South Newport. I also started running again.

Running had been a huge part of my life starting in my twenties; it was what helped me quit smoking and what helped me heal from an eating disorder during my college years. It is a favorite part of my stress-relief routine.

However, I hadn't run seriously in years. I started with ten minutes at a time whenever I felt up to it. To my surprise, running felt good again, right from the beginning. Eventually, those ten sporadic minutes grew to thirty minutes five times a week!

I shifted my perspective on self-care, letting everything I did for my body—from long runs to special pedicures—be an expression of the love and value I held for myself. I replaced some of my Netflix time with trips to Roger's Gardens, a plant and home decor store with beautiful displays that always inspired my mind to daydream. These activities left me feeling healthy, energized, and empowered. I was starting to see the person I wanted to be on the horizon.

I knew that I wanted that person to be led by faith. My faith has always been important to me, and when I was in the throes of grief immediately after Jack's death, I turned to God for comfort. Prayer became part of my meditations and walks, and I found comfort in those spiritual conversations. I know some people turn away from religion after a loss, blaming God for what has happened. For me, my faith was a source of comfort.

In this moment of recreation, I held a vision for expanding that faith. I began to read my Bible, the one I had owned for thirty years and never opened. Every morning I read a few pages and then spent a few minutes in prayer and meditation, pondering what I had read. This new routine, rather than looking at my phone and watching the morning news, decreased my stress tremendously. I talk more about this in Chapter Fourteen.

I started regularly attending St. James, the Episcopal church where we held Jack's funeral. Our family had attended only on holidays before Jack's death, and it felt good to lean into the community and the spiritual side of myself.

Another thing I did was rekindle my long love of outdoor adventure. I started with a camping trip to Pinnacles National Park with some good friends Bill and I used to backpack with. I thought this familiar group would be easy to slide back into.

Boy, was I wrong. It was so much harder than I expected. Bill and I had always teamed up for all the outdoor setup tasks, but now it was just me, Tori, and her friend.

The tasks proved too much: Set up two tents, arrange our gear, assemble the chairs, start a fire, prepare the food. It was overwhelming. Bill and I had developed a rhythm over the years, an unspoken division of labor that moved us toward a common goal. Now there was no rhythm. Every task felt new and onerous, another thing to do, manage, or delegate to Tori. I had to play worksite manager, figuring out how to do this without Bill.

I ended up sleeping in the back of my car, because setting up a second tent— just for me to feel utterly alone—proved to be too much. Bill had been such a large presence on past trips, always joking around and making everyone laugh with his stories. It was strange to not have this dynamic, and I didn't know how to relax and be comfortable. I was surrounded by the same people in a familiar setting, but the atmosphere felt so completely different.

Even worse, these wonderful people with the best intentions kept trying to pull me into conversations that framed this trip as my getting "back to normal." Ouch. When you've experienced traumatic loss, you know there is no such thing. There is "before" and "after." Their well-intentioned attempts only reminded me of how much I had lost. It was all still so fresh. On the way home, I nearly ran out of gas in a desolate area with no cell service. We barely squeaked by, pulling into a tiny gas station in the middle of nowhere after twenty minutes of driving on empty. I was used to Bill being in charge of such things, and I realized my brain was not paying attention to the details.

That trip truly tested the burgeoning new Julie. Immersed in a familiar environment, I found it difficult not to focus on what I had lost instead of what I was creating. My "nothingness" sure didn't feel like an opportunity when I was again with friends who knew me only by my old life. Being with this group of friends without Bill was uncomfortable. But I stayed. I put up the tent and prepared the food. I even talked a bit around the campfire, something that was a stretch for me in that circumstance. Looking back, I realize what a big deal that was—pushing myself to venture out of my comfort zone but just going through the motions.

When you embrace your new self, some discomfort is inevitable. Of course it is—*everything* is new. A loss this size makes the whole world foreign, and you have to learn to navigate it while trying on a whole new you! I know it is much easier to remain the same, to not change. The brain is actually wired to crave sameness. It takes effort and drive to create change, pushing against the natural wiring of the brain. So give yourself some grace. You are brave just for being here. Even though the first few things you do may feel uncomfortable and awkward, I encourage you to "fake it till you make it." It is actually proven that going through the motions of happiness, even when you don't feel happy, will improve your mood. It's like practice for your brain. Imagine who you could be if you embraced that truth for all the incredible feelings of this "new you" that you are creating.

The next opportunity to practice being the new Julie came unexpectedly. A water polo mom who introduced me to beach yoga had planned a hiking getaway with three of her friends, and one dropped out last minute. They offered the spot to me. I said no at first—these were recent connections whom I didn't know that well. But as I thought about it, I knew I had to go. Maybe being around new friends who didn't know the old me would actually be good for me. I was recreating myself! If the Julie I want to be leaned into her love of outdoor adventure, how could I say no? I made the call, and suddenly there I was in Utah, at Bryce Canyon National Park, with three almost-friends. I had never been there, and I was awed by the natural beauty. The absolute masterpiece of orange rock formations could have been sculpted only by God. As we hiked down the one-and-a-half-mile trail into the bowl of glowing orange and gold hoodoos, I felt the presence and awe of our Creator, as I always do when in such natural bliss. To this day, I am still moved when I think about that beautiful landscape.

The next day, we drove to Zion National Park, another new site to me. We hiked the Narrows, a beautiful yet challenging trail up a narrow gorge cut by thousands of years of churning water. Today that water is a shallow stream in the base of the gorge, dwarfed by the sheer cliff sides that tower above it. Making my way through that narrow pass, a tiny speck in the vastness of the world, was one of the most exhilarating things I've ever done. We took a break for lunch in the gorge, sitting on rocks and pulling out our makeshift picnic.

What happened next was otherworldly.

Suddenly, a host of butterflies and dragonflies zoomed around us, surrounding us in a whirlwind of fluttering rainbow wings. We sat still, warm in the sunlight, wrapped in our silent moment of shared awe. No words necessary. It truly felt like a dream. I knew immediately—this was Jack. Dragonflies were one of his signs to me, after all, I had shared this belief with these new friends before the trip but wasn't completely sure how they felt about "signs from our loved ones." For a blissful moment, I basked in his wonderful presence. Then the moment passed, and the dragonflies flew away. We came back to reality, and the other women expressed that they also felt a spiritual presence in those dragonflies. They agreed with me—Jack was here.

That mystical moment meant the world to me. I had joined the trip as an experiment of sorts; if I was going to embrace the new me, I had to try out things she would like, right? I had gone to new places with new friends and let them into my soul. All along the way, I was shown an abundance of beauty and majesty, and I didn't take a single moment for granted. I lived into the vision I had for myself, the person I wanted to be. And Jack showed up for this new me. It was like he flashed me that megawatt smile of approval.

Now, don't get me wrong. The trip wasn't perfect, and neither was I. We were flying out of Las Vegas, and we decided to stay there overnight on our way home. I spent an entire day drinking cocktails and crying into a beach towel by the hotel pool. Embracing the new me didn't mean I wasn't still sad. But I am so incredibly proud of myself for daring to embrace the new Julie, and taking that leap put me on metaphorical trails to Heaven. And those almost-friends from yoga? Sharing these formative moments bonded us into lifelong friends, sealed by the majesty of God's creation and the soft flutterings of Jack's presence.

So…who was I now? The new Julie was still a nurse. She was still a mom to all her kids: young or grown, physically present or spiritually present. But she was also healthy and happy, with routines in place to keep her body active and her mind inspired. She let self-care be a love letter to herself. She was a woman of faith. She was a passionate outdoorswoman who jumped at the chance to experience God in nature. And she was open to whatever the universe had in store. For me, that was enough.

Thanks to Jack, I was becoming the woman I had always wanted to be.

I believe that a major loss can often help you find a better version of yourself. In fact, there is a name for this: "post-traumatic growth." Research by psychologist Richard Tedeschi and his colleagues proves that a person who has lived through an extremely difficult situation, such as military combat, a natural disaster, or cancer, often experiences profound positive growth immediately after the tragedy. This growth is reported as enhanced personal strength and self-confidence, as well as heightened appreciation for their social relationships. My hope is that if you also have experienced a great loss or trauma, you will tap into this opportunity in the aftermath. A better self is waiting to meet you!

CHAPTER NINE

A Desperate Pilgrimage

As I practiced being this new version of myself, new opportunities opened up for me. One Sunday, I brought a seashell with me to church to place atop the columbarium that had held Jack's ashes. It was a special find from one of my beach walks where I'd talk to Jack. I showed it to Reverend Cindy, who had officiated Jack's funeral. She was happy to bless the shell, and it inspired an idea. It turns out, the scallop shell is a symbol of St. James the Great, the patron and namesake of our church.

Reverend Cindy asked if I would bring more shells and help package them with a small note proclaiming God's love and including the church's information. The idea was that parishioners could pick up these small gifts at church and give them out on their travels as little reminders and invitations. And Cindy asked me, a spiritual seashell collector, to help. What a perfect fit. I gladly accepted, and my daily beach walks became even more meaningful. I bagged up a few shells with the little notes and put a small "JG" on each card in Jack's memory.

This new me was now a contributing member of our church community, and that felt good.

This meant spending more time with Reverend Cindy, and a short time later, she asked me if I would be the Parish Nurse. The position was volunteer, and it required a seven-week training to earn a Faith Community Nurse Certification through the American Nursing Board. It was a big ask but an easy answer.

This church had given me so much love and support, and this new me wanted to be part of that community. I became the Parish Nurse, a role that gives me purpose and great joy. I saw being part of the ministry team as a great honor. It also helped me integrate into the community. Now when I went to church service and attended the fellowship after, so many went out of their way to say hello and chat with me. I found a church family and a sense of purpose, and I was so grateful.

I encourage you to find something meaningful and embrace getting more involved. I think of those people and opportunities that came into my life after Jack died as gifts from God; embracing them is my gift or thank you back to my Creator. This is my personal belief and it is what has helped me in the movement toward healing.

The next opportunity to grow my faith was a surprise. I signed up for a walkathon fundraiser for AFSP—the American Foundation for Suicide Prevention. My team consisted of me, my mother, and my friend Kim, each of whom had lost a teenage son. On the morning of the walk, we gathered around the memorial tree the organizers had set up at the starting line.

I tied a tag bearing Jack's name to the tree. He swayed in the breeze, surrounded by the names of other loved ones who lost their lives to suicide. I cried, from both the sadness I still felt and from the support of being a part of this beautiful club. It was strange to see his name there. I approached the booth that was giving out beads in different colors that represented different aspects of suicide. I took my white beads, the symbol for the loss of a child. I was not the only one. I also took some beads to give to Tori for the loss of a sibling.

Walking with the other Survivors of Suicide, my fellow AFSP walkers, was very emotional. Tears streamed down my face as I wondered if I would ever feel normal again. Yet, despite the sorrow, there was a comfort in being with my little team of three. I wasn't alone. I was a hiker who had already taken long beach walks to nurture my tattered soul. To walk with others in collective memory of our loved ones made sense to me. Not a club I ever wanted to be in, but here I was.

It was a fitting gesture for Jack too. He loved outdoor adventure, even better if he could experience it with friends. As I walked, my mind kept turning back to the day Jack was born. He had entered the world in such a dramatic way, as if to say, "Here I am, world, let's get this adventure started!"

Jack was almost eleven pounds at birth—a gigantic baby! I didn't have any medical conditions that would cause such a large baby, he was just naturally big. At two in the morning the sensation started, and I knew. I woke Bill to tell him we needed to go to the hospital, and he frantically gathered all our prepared items for what we thought would be several hours of labor. Bill got us to the hospital quickly—in the nick of time, as it turns out— then ran into the ER like all the sitcom depictions of a frantic expectant dad.

"My wife is having a baby! My wife is having a baby!"

The ER nurses looked at him and rolled their eyes. They see this scenario every day, and it is usually hours before the baby comes. But not my Jack. A wheelchair quickly whisked me up the three floors to the Labor and Delivery wing. I had to wait ten torturous minutes for the doctor, fighting the urge to push. Jack didn't even want to wait ten minutes! A few minutes and only two pushes later, Jack was born, purple-faced with broken blood vessels in his eyes from the force of a wild ride of a delivery.

Jack was so full of life, he sprinted into the world with the same speed and enthusiasm that would characterize everything he did. It also strikes me as I write this that he ended his life in the same manner, fast and with enthusiasm if you can believe that. He ran out onto that highway, waving his arms above his head, on purpose, almost the same way he hurled himself into that delivery room. This is so, so difficult to understand, but I have to give him grace and accept that this was his decision. He chose to leave this physical world for reasons not completely understood by anyone. But even at his lowest point, he was still my Jack, my wonderful, full-of-life, refuse-to-be-denied Jack.

I was becoming the person I wanted to be, someone who lived with the same zeal for experience as Jack. But still I found myself drifting back to memories of Jack's life, going all the way back to his birth. Even though his birth story is almost unbelievable, there were decisions I made that I later regretted, and I now found myself wishing I could change things. I wondered why I was even focusing on these past regrets when I had come so far up the mountains of grief. Once again, I gave myself some grace, reminding myself that healing does not travel in a perfect straight line. It's a twisting, up-and-down trail across mountains. Some days, I lived in peace, loving the person I was becoming. These were the uphill days, the ones where I scaled higher and higher up the Mountain of Recreation with the sun on my back.

And other days, I lay in bed, questioning this new life and desperately wishing I could give it all back and undo everything. I realize that these difficult days were also part of the healing climb. They are the natural dips in elevation that a trail takes as it winds its way up a mountain. If you are in this place, where you feel yourself backsliding into despair, take heart. It's all part of the healing journey. You can teach yourself to choose higher-level thoughts and allow those thoughts to empower you to continue up the trail.

As I progressed further up the mountain, I grew stronger. I learned to minimize those dips with techniques to train my mind. In the next chapter, I'll share how I met my life coach, Lisa J., and how she taught me the process to shift negative thoughts and reclaim my joy.

CHAPTER TEN

Relearning How to Soar

It promised to be a fun party. I didn't know it would change my life.

I walked into the home in my holiday best, cautiously hopeful of an uplifting night of Christmas cheer. Of course, I had an exit strategy. It was barely a year after Jack's passing, and the holidays were a difficult time of year. As I mingled, I scouted for the host of the party. She was an extremely good friend, one of my closest confidantes. In fact, she was such a sweet friend that she had gifted a copy of a personal development book to Bill last year, hoping to help him find some direction and get out of his funk. He didn't read it at the time, but I did. The book was *Mindset Reset*, written by an established psychologist and life coach named Lisa Jimenez. Let me tell you, I devoured that book. And as I scanned the room for my friend, I spotted her chatting with another guest. Suddenly, I recognized the guest from a tiny "meet the author" photo at the back of the book.

My friend was talking to Lisa Jimenez.

I walked over, and the three of us immediately connected. After a while, it was just me and Lisa. We chatted about the holidays, and I told her a little about Jack. She was very open and caring, but it was a party, and after a while we went our separate ways. Still, I was intrigued to talk more. I saw Lisa again by chance, at a store opening a few weeks later, and she invited me to lunch at her home. When I arrived, I was shocked to realize that Lisa's home was the exact home I had just walked by a few days earlier. A different good friend pointed out the house was where she would be leading her Bible Study. Two of my best friends knew Lisa J. and respected her as a teacher! I took that as a sign.

Lisa asked how I was coping and listened to my story. Then she told me about her Mindset Reset coaching program, which focused on helping people notice their automatic responses to frustration and trauma and teaching them how to choose different ways of thinking. It was exactly what I needed at the time. Lisa is also a Christian, and her coaching comes from a spiritual place without being overly religious. That really sold me—I believe that what she offers is based in truth. *And* the program included a weeklong retreat in Paris, France! It was a dream.

However, a week's vacation is hard to come by as a nurse, and I'd already submitted a week off for a friend trip that had fallen through. I couldn't get those work days back. Would you believe it, the Paris retreat was over those exact dates! Lisa and I both got goosebumps when we realized the coincidence—or was it God's divine will over me? I knew I *had* to do this program.

Hiring a life coach was the missing piece for me. The greatest gift I have received from the loss of my son is the focus on self-improvement, healing enough to one day help others in similar situations. I needed a major shift in my perspective. Life has its ups and downs, but Jack's death was such a devastating blow that, despite all the healing I'd done, I knew I wouldn't fully recover without completely reinventing myself. I realized that diving into a life-coaching program to retrain my mindset would change everything for me.

The program began with a questionnaire to hone in on my belief system. I learned that what we believe about ourselves is formed at a very young age, and this self-image usually remains in place for our entire life unless *we actively take steps to change it*. This fit with what I had learned from the Grief Recovery Method—that early losses shape our trauma responses, and we have to dig into past grief if we want to fully heal. This is Mindset Reset—reprogramming what we think, using self-awareness to shift our mindset and move into a higher level of being.

Let me be clear, I would not have been ready for this if I had not done the radical healing first. Private therapy got me open to the idea of talking through my trauma to move past it. The EMDR helped me overcome PTSD from the trauma of Jack's suicide and also the PTSD resulting from early childhood trauma that I had never explored before Jack's death. The Grief Recovery Method helped me to *process* the loss of Jack and six other losses from my past. It gave me hope that I could move forward without those losses weighing me down with every step. I had to get over the Mountain of Shock and scale the Mountain of Hope before I was ready to truly recreate myself.

Starting Mindset Reset coaching was like opening Pandora's box. Once I started peeking under the lid of my own psyche, all the limiting beliefs, trauma responses, and facets of my self-view came flying out. As I said, the program started with a questionnaire. I could see my entire inner world clearly laid out in front of me.

So much truth was right there within my answers in that questionnaire. On the first page, I saw my belief that there was never enough money. My family was always "house-poor" when I was a kid, and Bill and I had stretched to buy homes and cars we could afford only by sacrificing everything else. I was always telling my kids, "We can't afford it." On the next page: Happiness is a finite resource. If you've lost a great joy, it's possible that it was a pinnacle you will never reach again. In this corner: Some mothers who lose a child are so deeply consumed by grief that they believe their own lives cannot continue without that child, and this overwhelming love can tragically lead to their own death soon after.

But through all this self-reflection, one undeniable truth emerged:

I have the power to change the way I think about all of this.

It is amazing what self-awareness can do. Knowledge really is power. Together, Lisa and I worked on shifting my limiting beliefs and more. I practiced noticing these beliefs when they came up in moments of stress, acknowledging them as part of a worldview that no longer served me. I started to consciously create a new version of who I wanted to become. With repetition, those new thoughts started to feel real. They actually became what I now authentically believe. This type of coaching, and Lisa J.'s Mindset Reset Formula, was incredibly effective for me.

Now when I feel stressed over an expensive opportunity and "We can't afford it" comes up, I think, "I will make it happen." And I do. I have trained myself to think of money in terms of priorities—what I am willing to trade or how much I am willing to work for this opportunity—instead of defaulting into a sense of lack and impossibility. When I notice myself thinking, "I'll never be that happy again," I reroute that thought to "My best times are ahead." And it's true! My capacity for joy is growing, and I am understanding the power of gratitude with every passing day. My happiest day is always ahead of me, because as I keep expanding, so does my happiness threshold.

Now, the biggest reframe I had to create was this one: Even though for a very long time I believed, "The loss of a child is the end of a parent's life," I knew deep down that was a lie. An obvious one too. I have experienced so much since Jack's death. It is possible, however, to make this lie a reality as many do after the loss of a child. This belief can stick if you tell yourself it is true enough times. Interesting how stubborn the brain can be, even when faced with evidence that directly contradicts what it thinks is true. No matter how much inner work I had done or how many "good days" I was having, I just couldn't reframe this long-held belief about life ending when a child dies before its parents do. When I started to move away from this thinking and would be feeling okay, or even happy, I would slip back into guilt. I felt guilty for moving on. I felt guilty for feeling peace. But over time, I consciously chose to believe that my whole life is ahead of me and that I bring Jack with me into this new, joy-filled life going forward.

After EMDR, the Grief Recovery Method, and Mindset Reset coaching, I have disconnected from my trauma responses and learned how to shift them. I consciously choose not to let them run wild. I truly feel that I have unlocked a way to get to zero-point energy at any time. This series of different therapies and modalities each worked alone; yet together they brought me to this place of an open and clean slate, ready to receive something to fill in the void.

Do the work it takes to get yourself to this healing state, however long it takes. You may be surprised how quickly healing can come. I am proof that it can happen relatively fast. I am sitting here fewer than three years after Jack's death and writing a book about how I transformed myself—and giving you the information on how you can do this too.

I am not saying that what I did has healed me one hundred percent from the loss of Jack. I still have moments that overwhelm me with sadness from losing him. But now I have the tools to keep me from going down the rabbit hole of grief that can lead to depression and ultimately to disease. I now am able to give myself a moment, an hour, or even a whole day to be sad that Jack is not here. I can cry for his loss, but after the allotted time, I focus back on the fond memories and pull myself out of the sad state.

By focusing on the good, I am able to move to a higher level that brings positive feelings. I can now shift my thinking and tell myself that I don't have to remain in sadness. I can choose something new. This is something you also can learn. Practice how you wish to be and eventually it becomes part of who you are.

Mindset Reset coaching gave me another precious gift: a new dream.

A dream of a life with joy, happiness, freedom…and helping others achieve the same. A dream of helping people like me move through grief and reclaim their joy. And it started with becoming certified as a Grief Recovery Method Specialist.

Shifting my perspective on life after loss also shifted how I saw others' stories. Moms dying after losing a child? That's not cosmic justice. It's tragic. Parents, especially moms, often suffer unexpected and untimely deaths related to health breakdowns, whether physical or mental. You can die from unresolved grief.

Recent examples of this are seen in the untimely deaths of three famous women who had lost a child and died relatively soon after: Anna Nicole Smith, Sinéad O'Connor, and Lisa Marie Presley. This pattern is a real concern.

I saw my own mother's breakdown after the death of my brother; she fell apart and suffered emotional and physical ailments for many years. She survived, but she never really recovered. I don't want that to happen to anyone else. At the Paris retreat, I realized that I am uniquely positioned to help prevent some of these tragic outcomes. I know I have a calling to create my own business as a Grief Recovery Specialist. It takes action and purpose to move out of the cycle of self-destructive behaviors. I am standing strong for all of you who have lost a child—anyone who has gone through loss. I feel like Esther in the Old Testament saying, "I am called for such a time as this."

I knew after going through the program myself that it provided my best avenue for healing not only the loss of Jack, but all the major losses from my past. I want to bring that healing to others. I left the Paris retreat with a clear picture of my future business and some actions steps to get there, born of the truest expression of my unique soul and honed by Lisa's coaching and input from the other participants at the retreat. Grief recovery coaching will be my first new business. My intention is to lead groups in the Grief Recovery Method.

I've come up with some wonderful ideas that I'm confident will bring this healing to the world, including this book. The concept for this very book was born in that coaching program and is a vital part of realizing my purpose.

Just last week, I was visiting friends in Paradise, California, whose residents lost everything in the devastating Camp Fire a few years before. I met a lovely couple who were warm and engaging. We chatted over a few glasses of wine, and as the time went by, and the warm glow of alcohol set in, we started to open up to each other. When I told them I was writing a book about healing grief, the husband shared a heart-wrenching story.

He was passionate about antique cars, a hobby he had picked up from his father. They had amassed quite the collection over the years. He and his dad spent thousands of hours over many years lovingly restoring dozens of autos. After his father passed, this gentleman continued the tradition alone. These cars were precious beyond words to him. Then, in 2018, the Camp Fire raged through Paradise, and all of his cars were destroyed. There was nothing left of them.

This loss was so profound that he had not even been able to talk about it until our conversation (and several glasses of wine). And I, a mother who has lost a child to suicide, mourned with him. My unique healing journey had prepared me to see the unthinkable tragedy in his story. I knew from the GRM that all losses leave scars, and the size of the loss is personal to the one experiencing it. It doesn't have to be the loss of a person to forever change you. I understood the pain. I, uniquely, could talk this man through his grief as both a teacher and an equal. This was a confirmation in my eyes that I was onto something bigger than my own grief. I could step outside of my emotions to help others process their pain.

I am deeply committed to guiding people through the most challenging moments of their lives. This is my purpose, and I consider it a profound gift.

I believe that you, too, will experience a moment of clarity when your purpose becomes undeniable. You will rediscover your ability to soar.

CHAPTER ELEVEN

This Is So Jack

I rushed into the bathroom of the hotel, incredibly grateful to be out of the truck we'd hitchhiked in and away from the mountain we almost didn't make it off of. If I were anywhere else, I would have kissed the ground.

Our hike had started off like any other. We were excited to explore a new corner of the Sierra Nevada mountains. We struck out along the John Muir trail, just south of Yosemite, heading north into Evolution Basin. That area is known as the prettiest part of the Sierra-Evolution Lake region, and it was a perfect day. I was in my early thirties and particularly fit. Because I was an accomplished mountaineer, with several fourteeners and many other challenging peaks in the Eastern Sierra Mountain Range under my belt, I was confident in my abilities. Our whole group consisted of seasoned backpackers: me, Bill, Bill's father Ken, his younger sister, Sarah, and our friend, Tracy.

Bill and Ken were leading the group when disaster struck. Ken tripped, a tiny tumble onto the trail that seemed like no big deal. But that tiny tumble had dislocated his finger, on which he wore a ring. In the backcountry, this is a drop-everything emergency. A dislocated finger swells, and a swollen finger in a now-too-small ring could lead to amputation. The plan immediately changed; Ken had to head back to town (luckily he got the ring off in time), and our group was down two hikers. Sarah escorted her dad to the ER, so that left Bill, Tracy, and myself.

We continued on, but in the confusion, we lost our position. We climbed up a ravine that we thought was a shortcut marked on our map, but we were wrong. We crested the Sierras in the wrong place, far from the trail and any other hikers. We found ourselves in a large, raised-boulder field with steep scree sides. As we crossed the field, panic began to rise. It was getting dark, and we couldn't go back down the ravine we'd climbed before sunset.

Getting lost in this remote location can be life-threatening. We decided to keep going until we found a place to make camp, then reassess in the morning.

Even with our experience, we knew looking for a campsite without knowing which way the trail headed was nothing less than terrifying. At one point we had to descend down one of the steep slopes where there was no path. The entire surface was covered in a deep layer of loose pebbles and small rocks. Taluses and scree accumulate where snow comes down and fills the slope, which can be fun to jump down and slide with each foot, but can also be very dangerous as the trail becomes unstable. You can get seriously injured. Not a good place to be in when we had no way to get emergency help, plus no one knew where we were since we had gone off the trail. We had to make our way down with our heavy backpacks on. I fell hard on my butt, my pack adding weight to the impact. I was already a little panicked, and that fall pushed me over the edge. I had been tough up to this point, but now I felt tears sting my eyes. A real sense of danger set in. I was frustrated, scared, and exhausted, but we had to push on to find water and shelter.

Luckily, like a miracle, we found a place amongst the enormous boulders, with just enough space to pitch our tiny tents. A little stream of water bubbled through the rocks nearby. To us, it was an oasis. The next day, we were able to find our way back to the trail using a trail map and compass. We finished the hike, but because we descended at an unplanned trailhead, we had no way to get back to our car. We had to hitchhike.

A guy in a weathered pickup truck took pity on us and offered us a ride. Without hesitation, we threw in our gear in the back and climbed in. We were so ready to be off the mountain.

Now, this driver was a piece of work. As he flew down this rickety mountain road, we in the back seat bumped and swerved and twisted the whole way. The ride made me sick. Really sick. Suddenly, I had a thought. Was I sick from peak stress and the bumpy ride back to town...or was it morning sickness? Bill and I had been trying for a baby. We stopped for a pregnancy test on the way to the hotel, and I rushed into the bathroom. Three minutes later, I flipped over the test. I saw the strong pink line and immediately shed tears of joy. What an impossible, harrowing, elating rollercoaster of a weekend.

It was so completely Jack.

The moment a woman discovers she is pregnant, she is gifted the warrior mom spirit that creates an unbreakable bond with the baby and ignites the drive to nurture and protect that child at all costs. This warrior spirit intensifies as the baby is born and continues to grow with the child. Though the bond forged through carrying the child is certainly its own unique and beautiful connection, all parents have some form of warrior spirit that grows in them as they bond with the child. I believe that this spirit is an actual energy. I know I felt it from the moment I first learned I was pregnant with Joshua at the young age of fifteen. With Jack's pregnancy, I could feel from the beginning that he was one tough kid, and that my mama energy was roaring along with him. His life force and my warrior mom spirit were created at the same time and grew together from the very beginning.

The nature of energy is that it is never extinguished but transfers to a different form. *Why You Want a Quantum Physicist at Your Funeral*, a paper that changed my perspective on death and grief, explains that all of the energy that was created when the world was birthed is still present today. The earth is a biosphere that contains all this energy that has always been here and will continue to be here, just changing shape and transferring through all living things. I talk more about this in Chapter Fifteen.

This was such an aha moment for me!

Reframing my views on death in the language of conservation of energy made sense and gave me a feeling of relief. When Jack's heart stopped beating, his life force left his body. Yet I feel that energy remains in a changed form in the unseen quantum field. I find this information rings true with how close Jack feels to me at times or when something seems like a sign he is near.

Now here is where my theory gets a little more…theoretical. But it is based on my lived experience. I believe the same is true of the warrior mom spirit that grew with that child. That spirit is an energy, and just like all energy, it cannot simply disappear. It can only remain or change. So where does all that energy go? I believe it can actually grow into a passion that feeds your purpose in life. This force is a gift, fueling the drive to discover your life's purpose with the same unstoppable tenacity that it used to focus on the child.

I am awe-struck by how this has happened to me. I know my passion for helping others heal would never be so strong without my warrior mom spirit that grew with Jack, still residing inside of me. I refuse to let the energy Jack left behind when he ended his life be wasted or numbed down to nothingness. I am inspired now to take this energy force and use it to create something, and I want the same for you! Use the love energy that has transferred into grief from the loss and harness it into a passion for the good in the world.

Find your own God-given purpose, say yes to opportunities. God takes your "yes" and turns it into miracles that are beyond your imagination. Your warrior parent spirit will give you the passion and strength you need to embrace the miracles. All you need to do is accept this truth and let it fuel your ambition. Develop it into something that can honor your loved one. I am proof that the warrior mom spirit can fuel great things even after a child's death—and I am not the only one. I believe every human being is born with a specific purpose unique to us. The point of life is to discover that purpose and expand upon it, to put energy toward that purpose and see how it grows into something bigger.

If you're unsure of your life's purpose, self-reflection can help uncover it. Start by considering what brought you joy as a child. How did you spend your time? For me, playtime was all about having a house filled with baby dolls and playing doctor. These childhood passions eventually merged when I became a nurse in the NICU (Neonatal Intensive Care Unit), where I now care for tiny precious babies. I've always felt incredibly blessed to have this career. For a long time, I believed my purpose was solely tied to being a nurse, a good mom, and a wife—until Jack's death changed everything.

Now, with my grief pilgrimage, I have been given the gift of a new purpose. This is common—as I said in previous chapters, a major loss strips away so much more than just a person's sense of self. It breaks down our lives and our selves into the nothingness of pure potential, that zero-point energy. It's like a rebirth. Of course we seek new purposes—we are new people. We've climbed the Mountain of Recreation.

My new purpose is to help others navigate grief, and the warrior mom spirit that grew with Jack fuels that purpose every day. Nothing else matters as much for me as pursuing grief counseling and writing this book. I have had to give up some of the extras in life so I can allocate my time and resources to my personal development. My roots, fingernails, and floors are a mess, but that's fine. I would give up these things for Jack, so I can give them up for this purpose he gave me. That warrior mom spirit keeps pushing me forward.

The idea that an energy in you needs to be expressed through a purpose is not new. It is fundamental to many cultures around the world. One of the regions in which this has been demonstrated is Okinawa, Japan, a place that was decimated during WWII. The people of Okinawa still hold grief for what happened there, for so many lives lost. Yet this region's people have the highest rate of longevity in the world. Many Okinawans live to be over a hundred!

One of the fundamental aspects of their longevity is the focus on *ikigai*, or each person's individual purpose. *Ikigai* is something that you love, you are good at, for which you can be compensated or receive gratitude and the world needs. It literally translates as "reason to live." They believe that without *ikigai*, a person will die. There's clearly truth there, as many live happily beyond the century mark, carrying the community's grief with them along the way. I resonate with the concept of *ikigai*—without a new purpose, that warrior mom spirit in me would die. The part of me that was so fierce for Jack would die. I will not let that happen.

The process of writing this book has been cathartic but very emotionally draining. At the end of a tough writing session, I find myself empty of resolve, slipping back into behaviors that don't serve me anymore, like drinking wine too many nights of the week and eating whatever is in front of me. I've been rehashing memories that keep me in a sad place. When I found myself doing this, I gave myself a break, but then returned to more healthy patterns. Stepping into your purpose might bring up old feelings for you, too, especially if doing so, as has happened with me, requires you to relive and recount your loss and your pilgrimage to healing.

Fight against the pull to return to old patterns. The brain thinks sameness is safe, so it finds old patterns to be comfortable even if they are unhealthy. It is much easier to roll over and stay in bed than to get up and climb the mountain, literally and figuratively. I shift these moments by tapping into my warrior mom spirit with gratitude. Listing what I am thankful for about my purpose and this writing journey puts me into a happy state of mind. That warrior mom spirit pushes me up the mountain every time. Let your unstoppable parent spirit do the same for you. Focus on all the good things that living your new purpose gives you, and unleash your warrior parent spirit when the challenging or painful parts of that purpose weigh you down.

As I write this, I am at Bill's family cabin located at Fallen Leaf Lake, just south of Lake Tahoe in Northern California. A beautiful, little rustic cabin nestled in the woods next to Glen Ellen Waterfall and surrounded by majestic mountains at the edge of Desolation Wilderness. I came here to write—to use solitude, comfort, and inspiration to further my purpose and keep Jack's warrior mom spirit alive in me. This cabin is a place I have been coming to every summer with Bill for over thirty years, and so many wonderful memories flood my mind.

As I sit here, I can picture my father-in-law, Ken Green, the patriarch who died from brain cancer just a few years after retirement, sitting at the little kitchen table with the same strawberry-patterned tablecloth, eating his cereal across from toddler Jack. I can picture my older boys Josh and James sitting on the front porch in the chilly morning air, wrapped in an old army blanket, drinking hot cocoa to warm up in the first sunlight. They always shared the bunk bed in the back room. Years later, when Josh and James were grown, Jack and Tori shared the same bunk bed. I can still see them all, tucked in their little plaid blankets, exhausted from a day of kid adventures in the mountains.

Although years have passed, the memories are still fresh. I can picture Jack in the kitchen, laughing with his big, beautiful smile, Aperol spritz in hand, recreating recipes we learned on our Italy trip for the family, Madi, and Aunt Kit.

My first time at the cabin alone—just me sitting at the strawberry-covered table, writing what I can about Jack. I picture him as he would look now, his height filling the tiny room, and he is happy. I know he is happy wherever he is. In fact, I think I can feel that because he is right here with me. I am not alone after all. He is here, just as big and happy and lively as ever. And I am here, just as much his mom as I have ever been. His life force goes on, and so does the fierce part of mine that belongs to him.

His birth gave me the beautiful gift of a new warrior mom spirit, and his death gave me the even more incredible gift of a new life with a new purpose, one I couldn't live without the fighting spirit he grew in me. In some ways, this book is *our* purpose, and we are writing it together. I get up from writing and turn on the stereo to eighties music, dancing my own little "happy time" celebration.

This is me. The new me, exactly who she wants to be, full of purpose and peace. She's not perfect, but she's here, and she's happy. I have summited the Mountain of Recreation, and I can never go back.

You, too, have come so far. We're doing this together. We got past the difficult beginning, the Mountain of Shock, where every step took all the energy we could muster. We muddled our way through the death rituals and those first unthinkable depths of despair, lugging that impossible backpack up the trail. Then we moved to the Mountain of Hope, learning about therapeutic methods to help soothe our broken hearts and allow us to begin healing. We emptied that backpack and embraced the freedom of having nothing to carry up the mountain. We lost it all, so we could recreate it all and be anything we wanted to be.

Now we stand hand in hand at the peak of the Mountain of Recreation. We dared to allow devastating loss to become a gift. We endured the discomfort of trying on new versions of ourselves, and we found who we want to be. We discovered our new purpose along the way and allowed our lost warrior parent spirits to unleash their unstoppable ferocity into this new direction. We can bask in the sun on the summit, safe and warm in the surety of the life we were meant to live. If you're not there yet, don't worry. Remember, it's a slow, twisting, up-

and-down climb. You'll get there, and I'm always here with an outstretched hand.

As I stood on Recreation's summit, I thought I had reached the pinnacle of the mountains of healing. This was everything I wanted from the journey. And yet, I realized there was much more.

The funny thing about purpose is that it doesn't affect only *you*. It spreads your soul through the world, touching others and lifting them up. It contributes. As I continued pursuing my Grief Recovery dream, I found that helping others was the most healing modality of all. It turns out, there was one more mountain to climb, one I couldn't even see from the foot of the Mountain of Shock.

When you are ready, meet me at the base of the Mountain of Contribution. I'll be there, ready to guide you to heights neither of us even knew were possible.

PART 4:
THE MOUNTAIN
OF CONTRIBUTION

The Phoenix SHINES

CHAPTER TWELVE

Shine, Warrior, Shine

When I began writing this book, I started with an outline. I sketched out the bones of the Mountains of Shock, Hope, and Recreation, filling each leg of the journey with snippets of stories from my own journey up each mountain. It wasn't until I started writing that I realized I—and all of us on this pilgrimage to healing—have one more mountain to climb.

The Mountain of Contribution.

Helping others has been the final leg of my journey toward who I want to be. I always thought that the tired axiom "It is better to give than to receive" was just a trite phrase repeated by moms trying to raise unselfish children. It wasn't until after Jack died that I found the profound truth in this lesson. It feels good to do something for someone else, to be generous. I noticed that the more I gave of myself, the more joy and fulfillment I experienced. I was curious about why this was true.

According to a study by Deakin University, being generous— everything from giving someone directions to helping a friend move into a new house—activates the part of the brain that makes you feel pleasure. Plus, it releases a hormone called oxytocin that helps mediate social interactions and emotions. The higher your oxytocin levels, the more likely you are to give. So the more you do for others, the more you want to continue to do so. Like Ebenezer Scrooge in *A Christmas Carol*, we all can find true happiness in generosity.

It took Jack's death for me to understand this truth. I had lived for years feeling that I had to watch every penny. As I mentioned, I grew up house-poor, with every cent going to maintaining an appearance of wealth and a home we couldn't afford. We never had extra funds for a vacation, new clothes, or extracurricular activities. And we definitely never had money to give to others.

Looking back, I realize I recreated this scenario over and over in my life. Bill and I lived at the top of our means, keeping up the California fantasy of our perfect little family. Losing Jack shattered that fantasy and forced me to take a cold, hard look at myself and my life. After years of therapy and personal coaching, I now have a mindset of giving back. And my life is so much fuller.

I am also finding that the act of helping others is what creates self-actualization. In Victor Frankl's book, *Man's Search for Meaning*, he says, "Self-transcendence of human existence denotes the fact that being human always points, and is directed, to something, or someone, other than oneself—be it a meaning to fulfill or another human being to encounter." It is in this drive to help others that true healing occurs. So, the more you give to others, the more self-actualized you become.

Two months after Jack's death, I found myself standing at the doorstep of Robyne's Nest, my trunk packed with clothes. Deciding what to do with a loved one's belongings is an overwhelming task. Some people leave everything untouched as a shrine to the lost loved one, but since we were living in a rental house and would soon be moving to an even smaller apartment, that wasn't an option for me. I'm grateful for that constraint because it forced me to face the tough but healing task of letting go. Naturally, our family chose a few of our favorite, most sentimental items to keep. I also invited Jack's close friends to select any belongings they felt connected to as keepsakes. It comforted us to know that his girlfriend and friends had a few special mementos.

But what to do with the rest?

I wanted to do something memorable with Jack's clothes. I didn't want them sitting in a general donation bin, piled under all the castoffs of the neighborhood until they ended up in a landfill. I wanted them to go to kids of high school and college age. Kids like Jack. I was so lucky to find Robyne's Nest, a nonprofit that supports young adults who have aged out of foster care or otherwise don't have family support. I picked Giving Tuesday, the Tuesday after Thanksgiving that has become a traditional day to donate, hoping that the momentum of the holiday would help me let go. Still, I could barely greet the three ladies in the Robyne's Nest office, emotion strangling my voice. I directed them to the back of my Ford Flex and paused to say a prayer over the clothing. I prayed that the boys who received the clothing would have a full and happy life and that the clothing would bring the self-confidence that Jack always had. The three ladies had tears in their eyes as they heard the significance of this donation for me and for the ones who received it. I said another goodbye as we loaded the clothing into the office.

Later that week, I got a handwritten letter from Robyne herself. She told me about three boys that Robyne's Nest had recently placed in an apartment. One of the boys was starting college soon and desperately needed clothes—and he was just Jack's size. There was a kid out there who would dress like Jack! It was such a gift to know that Jack's belongings were being used well.

I thought a lot about that kid. He had no support without Robyne's Nest. Jack had everything a kid could need: a loving family, a nice house, a closet full of clothes, a full pantry, a passion and talent for sports, admission into a great school. Jack had every need met as far as I could see, and yet he suffered a mental breakdown and ended his life. The kids helped by Robyne's Nest have nothing, and yet they strive to live. Mental illness is so hard to understand! I wanted to support those kids in any way I could.

I started volunteering for Robyne's Nest—just in little ways at first, like collecting donations of specific food items to fill bags for the winter break from school. This way I could contribute but not have to interact with anyone. Then Robyne gave me such a beautiful gift, although I didn't know it was a gift at the time. She asked me to mentor a high school girl. What? Me, a mentor? I just didn't know if I was ready. But then Robyne shared that the girl wanted to go into nursing. The request was to meet with her a few times at her school and tell her about my education and career path. Now that I could do.

The night before I was to start the mentorship, I got an email that changed everything. It said, "Thank you, Julie, for your kind offer to volunteer. We are so excited for you to be doing career mentoring. The classroom is set for your fifteen kids."

WHAT?! I nearly slammed the computer shut. Fifteen kids?! No, I'm teaching one sweet, shy girl, not a room full of kids!

So, what would *you* do? What do you think I did? By now, you know that answer. I just said yes! I sent a few quick emails to get the lowdown. What did the other career mentors do? I knew I needed an outline—I couldn't just wing it. Typing out what I would teach each session made me less nervous about the idea. My biggest fear was looking stupid and disorganized in front of the girls, such an irrational thought but so common. I had practice leading small groups of grade school girls in Girl Scouts and Girls on the Run, but these were high school girls at a continuation school, so I was expecting some major attitude.

The next morning I arrived with my head held high and a carefully organized folder in hand. Fake it till you make it, right? With a gulp, I walked into the lion's den: a semi-dark room filled with tiny, uncomfortable desks and the intolerable whirring of a loud air conditioner. How do kids learn in such an environment? One by one the kids came in. Or should I say one...by one...by one. There were only three girls! Whew. I was relieved but also a bit perplexed. I found out later that career advice was optional, and my other twelve students had split early, before the main school day ended. I assumed that even those who showed up wouldn't care about education. How could they, coming from homes where even basic survival needs weren't being met?

I started with asking them to tell me something about themselves, which was met with eye rolls. But when I turned the conversation to career possibilities, they perked up. To my surprise, these girls were highly motivated to better their lives! They really wanted to hear about what I did and how much money I made. I realized they each expected nursing to be the quick and easy path promised in television ads for online schools that would quickly produce "Nursing Assistant" certifications. These ads play constantly on afternoon television, aimed at people who don't know better that this is not a good, long-term career path. The cost of living in California is high, and these girls would need a higher paying job than the nursing assistant positions a career academy would produce.

I knew I could help these girls.

I used the information they shared to plan for the next meeting, outlining different nursing programs, what jobs they qualified students for, and what the yearly income for each of those jobs would be. A week later, I entered that room with my head held high—for real this time. I gave those young women some different options of school and career paths, and we discussed the pros and cons, timeline, education costs, and projected salary of each. I explained to them that I was never a strong student in high school, that I struggled with dyslexia and a dysfunctional home life as well. I told them I was a teen mom who had a baby in my junior year of high school. I believe I helped them realize that the more challenging but better-paying path was achievable—if I could do it, so could they.

Over our six weeks of meeting together, I feel the girls got a good perspective on nursing, one explained in a way they could understand. And I got a sense of fulfillment. I knew I had made a difference, and I felt good about myself again. Being responsible for advising these three girls pulled me out of my sadness and thoughts of Jack. I was able to be one hundred percent present, and that was a wonderful gift.

That mentorship role was exactly what I needed. But sometimes when you say yes, it's not all roses. It might be HARD. I continued to volunteer with Robyne's Nest in bigger and bigger ways. One thing I did was sign up to help with a free music festival in the park. I was part of a team working in the Beer Garden, which meant I was surrounded by families on blankets, couples coming in for a beer or glass of wine, and lots of people already intoxicated and having fun. My family didn't do happy little things like this anymore, and I felt so alone.

I also realized that I don't have a tolerance for being around drunk men who think they are so clever with their beer-hazed, sloppy attempts at flirting. Ugh, too much. I wasn't ready for that big of an event; my wounds were still too raw to enjoy such a large, happy crowd. After checking that the crew had enough people to cover the venue, I left early.

But even on that tough day, there was a silver lining. The festival had vendor tables, and I met three people who became important contacts for my future health fair for Youth Mental Health. (I share this story later in the book.). Yes, I was in the beginning phase of planning something big, something I had never done before. I was giving back one small job at a time, and that was enough. In the small jobs, however, I found the courage to dream of doing more, a specific idea I'd had for some time and might eventually put in the works.

Volunteering is a wonderful way to get unstuck and free yourself from the repeating thought patterns of grief. It helps you open up to new opportunities. Not all the situations will be absolutely wonderful, and you may ask yourself, "What the hell have I gotten myself into?" I felt this way a few times. But I encourage you to do something that sparks a feeling of giving back, especially if it is to an organization that has helped you or works in the realm of the type of loss you have experienced.

That's how it started for me: I participated in two "Out of the Darkness" walks put on my the American Foundation for Suicide Prevention which helped me move forward. I felt sad at each, I cried a lot, but it also felt good to be with others who understood my loss. I can see now that doing these events set me up to be ready to say yes to the volunteer work. I encourage you to put yourself out there and find community events you can be a part of. This is the road to recovery and healing and also may just open new doors to places you'd never expect.

My friend Kim found the same truth in her own journey; her healing wasn't complete until she found contribution. Kim lost her precious son Connor in 2019 at age eighteen. Connor was diagnosed with a rare childhood cancer, Epithelioid Sarcoma, in 2015, but this is not what killed him. Remarkably, he fought and won his battle with this disease. Instead, Connor died in an accident. One of his greatest passions and true talents was motocross. Connor won many trophies and qualified to compete as a junior in the AMA National Championship. In an unexpected and tragic turn of events, Connor crashed his bike during this race on October 20th, 2019. He suffered internal bleeding from hitting his abdomen on the handlebars of the bike and bled to death on the way to the hospital.

This loss came so unexpectedly for my dear friend Kim. Her family means everything to her, and saying she was devastated doesn't even come close to the truth. Kim said that Connor was one of the most compassionate people she knew, not just because he was a great son, but because he treated everyone he knew like they mattered. He took the time to make everyone who crossed his path feel important. Connor was universally loved. He had nearly a thousand people in attendance at his funeral, and many of his friends still come around to visit Kim.

I didn't know Connor, but Jack did. They were in the same graduating class at Huntington Beach High School, class of 2019. As I write this, the day after a remembrance gathering for Connor, I am struck by the connections between Kim and me. Many of Connor's friends also knew Jack. Some had been to my house.

In Kim's house, I see many pictures of Connor similar to those I have displayed of Jack: the one when he was five years old in a Batman suit, the family vacation to Hawaii, the graduation photo with the orange and black tassels around the neck. The living room is also adorned with three giant portraits of Connor, created for the funeral service. These pieces are works of art, composed of hundreds of small pictures of Connor from his life, mosaics that magically produce an uncanny representation of his beautiful face. They were done by Lorne Cramer, the same artist who designed my book cover.

I interviewed Kim a few days before the fourth anniversary of Connor's passing. Her responses paint a picture of a mom still deep in grief yet trying to move forward. To this day, she carries anger and guilt about Connor's death. She says that the motocross organization left him without aid for twenty minutes, then paramedics were too slow in transporting him to the hospital. Kim and her husband were there, watching from the stands as Connor sat on the side of the track, seeming stunned but okay. Precious time wasted that could have made a difference in getting him to a trauma center.

Kim recalls thinking, "They're not moving fast enough. THEY'RE NOT MOVING FAST ENOUGH!" Kim still regrets not doing something about it at the time. This is one of the memories that haunts her.

Kim says the feeling of shock has never gone away; sometimes she thinks Connor is out of town on a trip and will come back. She swings between wishing she would die today and trying to continue with a positive life for the time she has left. She finds her joy in helping others. Kim started at home: she discovered purpose in supporting her daughter, who lost not only her brother but her best friend and hero, her everything. Kim says her daughter lost more than she and her husband did that dreadful day. Kim also found joy in hosting a yearly memorial dinner—a Mexican feast for Connor's friends to give them a place to reminisce about the boy they all loved. In helping them heal, Kim slowly heals herself.

Kim has also found purpose in giving back to the community. She is involved with the Epithelioid Sarcoma Foundation, where she continues making personal connections with other mamas in her shoes. She is currently planning a one-month stint as a volunteer English teacher for monks in Nepal. She wants to do something completely different that will allow her time to process the loss and reflect on her life going forward.

As Kim says, "I think it's a really, really tough road." The experience of child loss makes you feel like you are floating in the middle of the ocean on a tiny life raft. But finding ways to contribute gives that raft direction. Suddenly, you're not so lost. And if you find someone to sail that raft with you, you no longer feel so alone. She and I became instant friends the night she reached out to me, just one month after Jack passed and one year after Connor. We walked on the beach for three hours and shared our tearful stories with each other. By the time we returned home, we were bonded for life.

If you're not ready to give back, that's okay. I encourage you to go back to the Mountain of Hope, get the therapy needed to help you heal from your loss, to move forward to a point where you can open up space to reach out to others. Again, this pilgrimage isn't linear: You can hike back and forth, up and back down these mountains as many times as you need to. And you can't help others until you help yourself.

I suggest you go back and reread chapters of this book or try some of the tools you may have skipped before. But don't let yourself get stuck waiting to be perfectly one hundred percent healed. Perfect is not possible! You are on a journey of healing that will last a lifetime. So as soon as you're ready, raise your face to the mountain and take the next step.

Choose a charity that resonates with you and start by volunteering in a small way. You might be amazed at where this journey takes you.

You can find a list of organizations to help you get started on my website: juliegreenhealing.com. Pick one, make the connection, do the volunteer work, and then reach out to me and share your experience.

Remember when I had to think "fake it till you make it" to push myself to start mentoring those girls? I faked it, and I made it. I became a better, more confident version of myself as I stepped into the space of their needs. You *can* become who you choose to be. And that means you can decide to be someone who looks for joy in the world. You may have been programmed to think you must behave in a sad and depressed state after a loss, but you have the choice to change that perspective. Giving back was the biggest step for me in making this imitated joy real.

I've discovered that the more I cultivate this feeling, the more naturally it comes to me. In the next chapter, I'll share how I transformed myself into the person worthy of my purpose.

CHAPTER THIRTEEN

Extraordinary Life of Purpose and Joy

In the loss of my son, I discovered my purpose in life—well, for now, anyway. *Man's Search for Meaning* also says that man's meaning of life changes moment to moment. I am now finding my meaning through helping others heal from grief caused by loss. The writing of this book—although it's been difficult—has been a big part of my healing journey. Capturing memories and putting them on paper, making them part of history, is my stamp on this planet. The impact that stamp could have on others is part of my purpose. I am here to help others recover from grief.

Volunteering at Robyne's Nest opened an unexpected door for me: I was offered a space to teach grief recovery classes and lead grief groups. I was looking for a place to hold a practice informational session to a group of friends to tell them about my future business as a GRM specialist and introduce an idea—hosting weekend retreats—I had been considering.

Robyne offered a room at the Robyne's Nest office.

I was nervous to do the practice session—I have a fear of speaking in public. I'm comfortable teaching one-on-one or in small groups. I do it all the time in my work. But the idea of giving a presentation or speaking to a larger audience intimidates me, as you might guess from my terror of mentoring a big group of students. I practiced over and over, writing my talking points out on a yellow legal pad, accentuating parts with a green highlighter so I could glance at the outline to keep me on track. I filled the cozy room with little plaques offering affirmations like "I choose to be happy" or "My thoughts become my reality."

I felt confident in my delivery of the information, and everyone seemed engaged in what I was saying so I relaxed a bit. I ended the information session with a sound bath—one of the healing modalities that helped me and I plan to include in my weekend retreats. In just ten minutes, everyone was in such a deep state of zen that I had to wake up some people when the session had concluded. Everyone at the meeting took a brochure, leaving me feeling both empowered and validated. My ideas were strong, and the sound bath brought immediate healing. Partnering with Robyne's Nest gave me the perfect opportunity to practice sharing my future business ideas.

Sound baths were just one of many healing modalities that supported me on my journey. As you have seen, it took a blend of various therapies to help me open my heart to joy once more. This combination inspired the next step in fulfilling my purpose: launching my business as a Grief Recovery Method Specialist.

The curriculum, delivered through eight weekly sessions, offers a powerful, action-based approach to healing from life's deepest heartbreaks. By the time this book is published and you're reading it, I will be well on my way to helping others reclaim their joy.

For many of us, our responsibilities didn't stop with our loved one's death, and we don't always have the luxury of time to slowly get back to our daily activities. Many people need to go back to work, or take care of their families, or jump into the legal logistics that accompany a loss. For these people I can offer the Grief Recovery Method at an accelerated pace over four weeks time, doing two sessions a week with at least three days between each session. This pace gives enough time to do the homework while speeding recovery so they can get right back to their responsibilities.

My Golden Shell Formula Weekend Retreat is another exciting business venture. This idea emerged from the Paris Mastermind, where I devised a plan to enhance the healing process. These retreats are designed for those who need to undergo profound healing quickly to perform effectively in high-level roles at work or home. I envision a four-day intensive curriculum that combines proven therapeutic tools and modalities for a transformative weekend of healing. The aim is to offer an immersive experience, incorporating many of the techniques that have helped me, so clients can strengthen their ability to function despite their grief. This program will be tailored for clients who have completed the four- or eight-week sessions and are looking to further deepen their healing journey.

I'm envisioning four-day intensive retreats that bring together proven therapeutic tools and techniques in a focused weekend experience. This immersive program aims to help clients strengthen their resilience and ability to navigate life despite their grief. Stay tuned for updates on The Golden Shell Formula Weekend Retreats at juliegreenhealing.com.

Becoming certified in The Grief Recovery Method, launching The Golden Shell Formula, writing this book, hosting mental health fairs, and taking on speaking engagements—these are all parts of my new dream. They represent the pieces needed to complete the puzzle of my purpose-driven life.

Finding my purpose and starting to give back marked the final ascent of my long journey to healing. Now it's your turn to discover yours. I found that the nudges and opportunities that guided me came as I walked my own healing path. I'm thrilled that these signs led me to my new passion and purpose: helping others navigate their own healing journey.

How will you give back?

I encourage you to take each step one at a time, add the practices I have outlined in this book or others you may have found that work for you, and keep moving forward toward finding your own purpose in life. Everyone has a God-given talent or purpose that is needed in this world. You may think that your talent is not as significant as someone else's, but this is not true. We are all needed to make this world a beautiful, healthy, and functioning society.

I do have one caveat to this calling: Do not let your drive to help others deplete you. You cannot be the contribution you want to be if you are overtaxed. When I started volunteering and daring to dream of a life helping others find the healing I knew was possible, I saw how easy it can be to get lost in my exhaustion. I knew I had to keep my own cup full so I had energy to give to others. So I did two things: I cut out commitments that did not further my self-improvement in service of this purpose, and I set time aside to focus on myself.

Sometimes prioritizing only what builds you up means cutting back and saying no. I call this time the "chrysalis of self-improvement." Just like a caterpillar must enclose itself in a hard outer case to transform into a butterfly, you must protect yourself from things that will sap the vital energy you need to transform. That means taking on opportunities that will guide you in the direction you wish to go while pulling away from that which no longer benefits your new self. For example, I started stepping back from work at this time. And I love my job— helping little babies survive and thrive. I am truly fortunate to have a job that allows me free time between shifts to pursue my ambitions.

If you do this, you may alienate people who are used to relying on you to support their agenda, but that does not matter. True friends will stick with you and be happy to see you healing, taking care of yourself, and transforming into a better version of yourself.

Next, I made my self-improvement a priority. I wanted to be worthy and capable of my own big dreams! I started with a vision board, practicing goal-setting and visualization. Yes, many of those goals were community-focused, but they were always led by my own passion—what would make *me* feel happy and fulfilled. I also splurged on two retreats with my life coach, Lisa J. Again, the breakthroughs I had at these retreats equipped me to serve others, but I ultimately attended for me. I wanted to grow into someone worthy of my purpose, and I was willing to invest in myself to get there.

One of the most wonderful benefits of Lisa J.'s retreats was the travel. Putting myself in a completely different place physically became an easy catalyst for putting myself in a different place mentally. This was so freeing and eye opening! It reminded me of the Rick Steves tour Jack and I did in Italy in 2018. That trip opened a new perspective in both of us, a bonding experience that could not be matched. Attending these international retreats reawakened my passion for travel and reminded me of its profound impact. Now I am passionate about continuing this tradition with Tori and for myself. If you can travel on your healing journey, do it! I encourage you to step out of your everyday life whenever you can. Even if all you can manage is a walk in a different part of your own town, put yourself out there. I have found that discovering new perspectives is needed in the healing process.

Discovering a sense of purpose required uncovering the version of myself capable of living that purpose fully. Thus, self-improvement became a necessity—it was clear I had to grow to respond to the calling within my soul. What emerged along the journey was truly surprising.

Somehow, over the course of this multi-year pilgrimage, I became a leader. Yes, me, the girl terrified of speaking in public.

I started taking on roles like running events, mentoring teens, teaching classes, and serving the church as a Parish Nurse. Each "yes" to a new challenge fostered growth, transforming me into someone the community could rely on. Today, my writing a book or launching a business surprises no one but myself.

Saying yes to helping others feels natural now, and leadership is unexpectedly fulfilling. Organizing and running the church's quarterly health checks—where members seek guidance and support—has brought me immense satisfaction. I feel like a trusted figure in the church community. Building these connections has become a cornerstone of my mental well-being.

At work, stepping into a leadership role opened up new opportunities. When a position on my hospital's Bereavement Committee became available, my colleagues encouraged me to volunteer. They recognized my growth and my passion for grief recovery. This role aligns perfectly with my goals in The Grief Recovery Method program and has expanded my capacity to live my purpose. As I've grown, more opportunities to serve have come my way.

One day, Reverend Cindy suggested that I hold a health fair at St. James. I was overjoyed! This was exactly what I had been wishing for: a way to honor Jack while helping other kids his age with the same mental health struggles that took him. My eyes welled with tears as I realized the significance of this opportunity.

While doing a health fair is part of my role as the Parish Nurse, I was excited to bring my "I am that mom" message to this health fair. I started picturing myself standing in front of a gathering of people, telling my story and sharing the reason why I staged this event. Even though all of the other health fairs in the area were focused on adult health issues, this would be different. This one would be focused on mental health for youth.

Historically this has been a touchy subject. It's difficult to talk about suicide. It's challenging to talk about mental health. But we must talk about hard things. Talking about these issues actually lowers the risk of suicide. So, here's my chance. I'm ready. I'm up for this. Let's go.

I had never organized an event this large and really had no idea what it would take to put together a mental health fair. I asked one of the parishioners for help, and I hit the jackpot. Lynne did fundraising for a living, so she came with a wealth of knowledge on the topic. We started meeting at the Corner Bakery to hash out the plans. I marveled at how in sync we were and how our ideas flowed so effortlessly. We met for five months to organize and execute the first ever Mental Health Fair specifically for youth in Orange County, California.

At the same time, I met Anne Hyde Dunsmore, a woman who did fundraisers to bring awareness to the mental health of veterans. "Stop SuiSilence" is their motto, a portmanteau of suicide and silence. The meaning of this is that by getting someone with suicidal thoughts to talk about those feelings, to break the silence, the risk of their going through with such an act decreases by a large percentage.

Anne graciously offered to meet with me for ideas on how to run a mental health fair. When I walked into her office, I could see she was a busy lady. Her foundation, Angel Force

USA, is her passion project, which helps ex-military with the emotional healing veterans sometimes need after serving our country. Anne carved out one hour to spend with me. By the end of that meeting, she had come up with the name of my health fair, Love and Listen. It was perfect. I left her office with my marching orders and a heart overflowing with gratitude.

So many people began to show up and help me! First, an artist friend, Georgeanna Ireland, let me use her work of art, *No Leaf Clover*, as the background for our signs. She had created a stunning mixed-media painting in the shape of a heart— perfect for Love and Listen. I made a list of vendors I wanted to invite, focusing on what I call the "Five Pillars of Mental Wellness": good nutrition, proper sleep, exercise or physical activity, socialization, and mind rest. I felt fortunate to enlist a stellar representative for each of these areas. The vendors set up tables on either side of the beautiful Spanish-style courtyard at St. James Episcopal Church, each offering information and little giveaways geared toward teens and young adults seeking knowledge on mental wellness. A musician friend played live music which brought a lively, festive feeling to the event.

I wanted fun yet nutritious food but was on a budget. I knew pizza was sure to draw some kids, so I balanced that comfort food with veggie cups and fresh fruit skewers. Can you believe they were just as popular as the pizza slices? Next I arranged for two friends to run a mini-meditation room—fifteen minutes of stretching, meditation, and a sound bath—simply as an introduction into the wonderful benefits of quieting the mind through these practices. This was a big hit! I think people are looking for ways to quiet the mind, which does not always come naturally in today's high-volume, digitally enhanced world.

Tori and her friend ran a fun photo booth with a cute barnyard theme. But the most popular station was definitely the puppy corner. I booked a pet therapy foundation, Orange County Allies-Paws, to bring therapy dogs to the fair. Under the shade of the large magnolia tree off the courtyard, people played with Golden Retriever puppies and enjoyed a perfect moment of stress-free joy.

Finally it came time for me to speak. I thanked the vendors and volunteers and gave a short synopsis of why I had planned this fair, why I spent so many hours organizing and setting up the event.

"If we reach even one person today who needs help, this fair will have been a success." I paused and smiled out onto the small crowd of young people. "If you are experiencing any kind of emotional distress, you don't have to suffer in silence. You are not alone. We care and we can help."

Although we barely had thirty people attend this first event, I felt the fair went well—everything I had envisioned came together in a very meaningful way. Even with my fears and insecurities, there I stood, holding a mic, all eyes on me, speaking a clear, concise message of hope! I was proud of myself, and I felt like Jack was standing right next to me the whole time, arm draped over my shoulder, cheering me on. His ashes were fewer than a hundred feet from where I was standing, in the tiny chapel just inside the big doors to the sanctuary where church service is held.

This was the moment I pictured in my mind's eye when I first became the Parish Nurse: to provide a place of safety where kids can get some information that could save them from ending their life. I am more committed than ever to host this fair as an annual event and have even more kids attend the next year.

In the almost three years since Jack's death, I have become unrecognizable.

As I said before, and it warrants repeating, I died when Jack died. Life as I knew it ended the second I heard those never-to-be-forgotten words. I can't pretend that my life will ever resemble life before his death; it just cannot be. I accepted this at some point. But I have made this new life even bigger and better. I have made *me* better.

I can honestly say I feel happy most of the time. I know it is hard to believe this can be true, but it can. Trust me, it can. Now, every time I pass a photo of Jack, I don't think about his absence. I look at him and think how proud he is of what I am doing. I feel like we are working together to keep his energy alive by giving back. Even when I do something as small as hold a door for a colleague or let someone go before me in the checkout lane at Trader Joe's, I feel good, and I know Jack is proud of his mom.

I get to live an extraordinary life of purpose and joy. And you can too. In the next chapter, I share how this extraordinary life led me to a deeper connection with God and my spirituality.

CHAPTER FOURTEEN

Heights of the Human Spirit

Since Jack's passing I have such a strong connection to my spirituality. It is what has gotten me through this most difficult time of my life. Losing my precious son, having my heart ripped out, feeling alone…I believe there's just no remedy to heal that except through God. The pain of such profound loss, the loss of a part of me, I could not have navigated without this higher power leading me through. And that relationship has changed me into a giver. The core of my soul is contribution. I just want to give back. I have transformed myself into someone who lives for contribution, and in this new way of being, I have felt myself draw closer and closer to God. It turns out, giving back is not just moral but deeply spiritual.

It says in the Bible that generous giving will be rewarded. Corinthians 9:6-8: "Remember this: Whoever sows sparingly will also reap sparingly, and whoever sows generously will also reap generously." I have certainly found this to be true. Our spirits thrive in giving and generosity. It makes us feel good. The more I give, the more I seem to somehow have. When I opened my heart to giving, the result is that my heart has grown ten times in size. The more I give, the bigger my heart gets and the greater capacity it has to heal. Generosity will increase your heart's capacity for healing, too.

My understanding of God has transformed profoundly. I have believed in a higher power my entire life; I can't recall a time when I didn't have faith in an all-powerful Source. Since Jack's death, I feel this power walking beside me in everything I do.

This profound feeling of God's presence has inspired and empowered me on the Mountain of Contribution. By tuning into the opportunities that present themselves, I feel connected to Jack's spirit. Now that Jack is fully spirit, I connect with him by living in the moment and having gratitude for everything, even the little things. Look for your loved ones where they are, not where they aren't. They are no longer in the physical, so looking for them there can bring disappointment, frustration, and sadness. They are in spirit...so look for them in spirit.

As I mentioned in Chapter Eight, I am committed to reading the Bible for the first time in my life—cover to cover. I'm surprised I haven't read it completely through before. It just never occurred to me to take this on. I want to have my own understanding of what is written in Scripture and the historical timeline of events. The Bible I am reading is the Life Application New King James version. I enjoy that each lesson has some words of explanation on how it relates to my life in today's times. I read a few pages each morning and then write one journal page and pray or meditate for a few minutes.

Some of the stories in the Bible took me by surprise—I had no idea it could be so brutal! Yet, when I think about it, today's world can be just as harsh; human behavior hasn't changed much over time. The Bible offers countless examples of both good and evil, as well as numerous lessons on the power of contribution.

Look at the story of Moses: He was born into slavery and became one of the greatest leaders in all of history because he gave all of himself to helping others. He allowed God to work through him to lead his people out of slavery and into the promised land. Moses was not a perfect man—no one man is perfect except Jesus—but his example is extreme in how one person can make such a profound change and difference for many others. This is how God works—He works through us to make change for the good, and He rewards that contribution.

A recent Swiss study found that people who planned to spend money on other people reported higher levels of happiness than people who intended to keep the cash for themselves. So there is a benefit from doing something for someone else; it gives you a sense of purpose and well-being. This must be the reward that God was talking about, the actual physical reward of the feel-good hormones being released in our brain when we contribute. God created us and so He planned this happy juice to be released when we help each other. That is so awesome.

Even though I choose this Christian denomination for myself, I respect and honor all expressions of faith. It is so personal to each individual; who am I to judge what others believe?

What is important is having some form of spirituality. An intact belief system is vital to good mental health and aging in a healthy way. According to The McKinsey Health Institute, "Spiritual health encompasses having meaning in one's life, a sense of connection to something larger than oneself, and a sense of purpose. Finding this meaning is associated with strong mental, social, and physical health." The connection to a power greater than yourself is needed for spiritual wellness, allowing you to feel at peace with life even in the toughest of times. Mind, body, spirit all need balance to be healthy. So many people neglect the spiritual aspect of this triad of needs. Improving your spiritual life can contribute to the healing process.

If you lack spirituality or if you are angry at God and reject religion at this point, I do understand. It does sometimes happen after trauma, especially child loss. You might wonder, "Why did God let this happen?!"—a question most people in our situation ask themselves. I did. I was able to come to terms with it in my own way.

Jack and Tori had both been acolytes (helping at the altar during the service) at our church in Napa. They did it begrudgingly, but I could see how it gave them a feeling of belonging and connection. Their youth program planned a mission trip with an organization called Sierra Service Project, and both Jack and Tori went. They traveled to Chiloquin, Oregon, with the church group to help build and repair structures at a reservation for the Klamath tribes who live there.

When the kids returned from this mission trip, they told me how meaningful it was to them, how helping others really gave them a boost of the "feel good" hormones and a sense of pride. Sierra Service Project requires participants to experience a bit of the deprivation of the people they serve, so they can understand and sympathize with a little sliver of their experiences. Even after sleeping on the floor and eating only peanut butter and jelly sandwiches for lunch every day, my kids came back happier than when they left.

Jack told me that he got so much from this trip, he understood how we are here on this earth to help one another and to see where God is present in all things. I can picture the kids sitting on the living room floor of our Napa home, gushing about how proud they were of themselves for using power tools and really making a difference in the progress of the projects. Both kids said they wanted to go back the next year, although we moved the next summer to Huntington Beach, so they never did go again.

In the summer of 2023, nearly three years after Jack's death, I received an email from the youth pastor of that Napa church. The email was an invitation to the church service after that year's mission trip, when the church would recognize the kids for their good works and present awards, including the "Jack Green Memorial 4x4 Challenge." I had no idea such an award existed. Apparently, the year Jack went to Chilaquin, he made a spectacle of the pb&j lunch. In true Jack fashion, he made the most of a tough situation and turned a sad lunch into something fun for his friends. Instead of eating just one sandwich at a time, he stacked them four high and ate a single monster sandwich in several huge bites. The camp counselors captured this with a photo, and a tradition was born. Each year the ante is upped, and this year's winners ate a thirteen slice pb&j sandwich! I was honored to attend the welcome-back ceremony and place the lanyard with a plastic peanut butter and jelly sandwich on each kid's neck. It was just *so* Jack.

Focusing on contribution opened a portal to receive the miraculous, the supernatural, the spiritual side of living. My deeper connection to God makes me feel more connected to Jack. He is with me through all of the wonders of living this human experience, which is to experience the supernatural, the oneness with all of humanity, and the spiritual realm.

So where do I go from here? What could be next? These were the questions swirling around in my head at this time. I was surprised to realize the answer actually came to me.

The year after Jack's death, I was on a wellness retreat in Tecate, Mexico. One night, I found myself alone in this cozy room lined with old books. I can still smell the leather and binding glue. A movie was playing in the background: *Walking the Camino: Six Ways to Santiago* (2009). There in the darkness, I found out about the Camino, a hiking trail through Spain. It is a pilgrimage to the place where St. James the Apostle's bones are thought to be buried, a treasured rite of Catholics and other spirituals for centuries. The Episcopal church that I belong to, the church where Jack's ashes are buried, is St. James The Great in Newport Beach California.

Remember how I first started volunteering at St. James by giving out encouraging messages on seashells, because the seashell is the symbol of St. James and one of my personal symbols for Jack? As you have seen, I am also an avid backpacker. The coincidences were too many to ignore. I thought to myself, "I think I have to do this!"

As if the signs weren't clear enough, I later learned that Rick Steves, the travel expert whose Italy trip Jack and I had taken together all those years ago, had a part in the rerelease of the film *The Way*, probably the most famous movie about the Camino de Santiago. The trip with Jack is a highlight in my memories, a most wonderful mother and son time together that taught me the importance of traveling to other cultures. I began to see the Camino as an extension of that trip with Jack, complete with seashell symbols and the association with our church. Everything seemed to line up and point in the direction of me doing this.

The last piece of the puzzle was meeting my friend and mentor, Betsy. She is one of those dear people that God has placed in my life since my Jack died. Our stories line up almost too perfectly—she also lost a son named Jack. We met for the first time at a seaside restaurant, adjacent to my favorite sea glass beach. We shared our stories over good burgers and beer. I felt an immediate sisterhood with her—she wears a tattoo of JACK on her forearm with the scallop shell, a symbol of the Camino. How could I not adore someone who shares so many of the same experiences, a love of hiking and IPAs.

I met Betsy through a mutual friend: She is an extraordinary human being, and I was immediately drawn to her as a mentor for navigating life after loss. Betsy is a retired school teacher and wears the rugged good looks of a life lived in the Southern

California sun, deeply tanned in her seventies with a mane of gray and white hair. She is easygoing yet stylish, impressively fit, and has a beautiful big smile that makes its way to her twinkling kind eyes.

Betsy has endured many losses in her life—that of seven close family members over a forty year period—but the hardest by far was the loss of her adult son, Jack, in 2016. She had a special relationship with her oldest boy of three children. Betsy has done the work to heal her broken heart enough to put her focus on other things that give back to the community and also enough to have a sense of joy in her life. She loves to laugh, and this is contagious; you can't help but have a good time in her presence. She embraces life to the fullest, which is exactly what I aspire to do, so I seek out time with her whenever her busy schedule permits.

Betsy's son Jack was a licensed mariner who spent six months out of the year at sea. A Laguna Beach native, he had a love of the ocean. He started surfing at age four! While on leave from a job out at sea, he was riding his bike with a friend to go to dinner. He was struck by a speeding teenager. The eighteen-year-old hit Jack in a residential zone driving ninety-five miles per hour. The boy had just purchased a previously owned Audi and was showing off to a friend how fast it could go, while also texting, so he never saw Jack before it was too late. Jack was thirty-one years old with so much life to live ahead of him.

Betsy says Jack was one of those people that others were drawn to, with a "larger than life" personality and presence. From one of the pictures in her home, I recognized a tall, handsome man with Betsy's tan skin, brown hair, and same, big beautiful smile. Betsy loaned me one of Jack's jackets to wear as we walked to a seaside restaurant the first time I came to her house for a visit. As I slid into the jacket, I immediately realized what a big guy Jack had been. Although I never knew her Jack, I somehow felt connected to him being with Betsy that evening.

On the night of Jack's death, Betsy received a phone call at 2:30am from a detective with the Santa Cruz PD. When he introduced himself she thought, "Oh my gosh, what has Jack done now? Will he lose his mariner's license?"

The detective said, "I'm sorry to tell you...your son was killed by a speeding driver."

She told the officer that it wasn't a funny joke, and he should never tell a mom that.

The detective replied, "I'm sorry but it's true. Your son is dead."

She handed the phone to Jack's dad and screamed. Betsy said she always thought the howling of a bereaved mother was an overdramatized movie stunt. Now she realizes it is an all-too-real primal scream that comes from deep within. She said it was totally unexpected, out of character, and uncontrollable.

Betsy was in shock for a couple of months. She couldn't take a deep breath, and everything was foggy. She doesn't remember who attended Jack's memorial paddle out or the following celebration of life. She also said something interesting: She emitted a new and different personal scent, as did her other son. According to the PubMed Central website, the skin emits a particular aroma when under extreme stress as a nonverbal form of communication.

Betsy recognized she needed professional help. The week after the funeral, she contacted a counselor. She said Jack wouldn't want "Momma" to get lost in grief. In addition, she attended a support group for parents who suffer the death of a child, The Compassionate Friends (TCF). This group helped when she needed it the most, and she made connections with other moms who shared her loss. Betsy still attends the once-a-year candle-lighting ceremony they sponsor at Christmas time.

Walking the Camino de Santiago was part of Betsey's healing journey. She did her own pilgrimage—literally. The year after Jack died, she did one full solo trek (five hundred miles) on the northern route across Spain. She arrived at the Santiago de Compostela Cathedral on the first anniversary of his death. She has also done two other shorter Camino pilgrimages. Knowing that she did the full Camino as a solo pilgrim in her sixties gives me courage to also attempt this trek next year.

Betsy says she knows that God has given her the strength to face the rest of her life without her child.

"He has provided me with a family, friends, and a faith which, combined, have made me the better person I am today."

I see myself in so much of Betsy's story, and I want to embody her easy joy and zeal for life. If she can do the Camino, so can I.

I've planned a solo journey for this fall, and by the time you read this chapter, I will have completed my five-hundred-mile trek. I believe this pilgrimage will offer a sense of closure in my journey through grief. As I mentioned earlier in this chapter, there's a golden thread connecting these experiences for me. Collecting shells was part of my early therapy, and sharing these shells with little messages of hope became part of my work as my church's parish nurse. Then I learned that the scallop shell is the symbol of St. James, the patron saint for whom my episcopal church is named. I was already awed by this connection, but the coincidences don't stop there. It wasn't until after I committed to walking the Camino that I learned it is a pilgrimage to the remains of St. James! The path is marked by golden shells guiding travelers to his cathedral in Santiago, Spain. That golden thread has beautifully woven the pieces of my healing journey into a unique tapestry.

Then I met Betsy, who also lost a son named Jack and walked the Camino in his honor, and realized that Rick Steves, who guided Jack and me on a tour, featured the Camino on his travel show. The connections deepen. Rick and his girlfriend at the time, Trish, who was our tour guide, reached out with comforting words after hearing of Jack's passing.

I feel the Holy Spirit's presence in my life through these beautiful connections. The warrior mom spirit that grew in me with Jack feels like an aspect of the Holy Spirit, guiding me through life with divine insights since Jack's passing. It's important to recognize the golden threads in your own life. Seek out coincidences and moments of magic, and you'll find the Holy Spirit working in your life. Follow these signs and see what wonders unfold for you as well.

CHAPTER FIFTEEN

A Whole Soul, A Whole Universe

There is nothing quite like taking in the world from the peak of a mountain. The avid hiker in me loves the effort of the climb itself, along with the twisting turns as you snake through forests and over streams, then basking in the sun's glow from the summit is the epitome. In that moment, you are part of nature, part of something so much bigger than yourself. Everything is connected, and everything is in harmony, including you. It is a spiritual experience at the top of that mountain.

The afterglow may in fact be my favorite part of a long, hard hike. After all the strenuous activity, all the moments where you have to push yourself to crest one more ridge, the day comes to an end, and you get to enjoy the victory at the peak with your friends. It's a time of rest, reflection, and connection.

One of my favorite hikes was Bill's and my attempt of the Kaweah Queen, a stunning and colorful ridgeline deep in the center of Sequoia on the spur of the Great Western Divide in Southern Sierra Nevada. It is one of the toughest trails in the

Eastern Sierra mountain range. We did it with a few friends, including my best friend, Tracy. The hike itself was majestic, but when I think back on that day, I find myself reminiscing about all of us in the back of our friends' pickup truck, comparing foot damage after the grueling hike. We had parked in the lot of a small mountain general store, drinking cold beer and blasting U2's "Beautiful Day" off the giant sequoias that surrounded us. Our group of five felt a bond in the difficulties of our great adventure. The tough hike had connected us, and spending a few hours in that parking lot felt like basking in that connection, much like we had basked in the warm sun at the peak we had labored so hard to reach.

Along my pilgrimage from grief to joy, I experienced the same feeling. Though metaphorical, my journey through grief is the hardest hike I have ever done or will ever do. There were moments when I was certain I could not take another single step, yet take one I did. Then another, then another. The path had its ups and downs, and it took everything in me to make it to the summit, but the effort was so worth it. Standing atop the Mountain of Contribution, I am in awe.

It's hard to believe that so much beauty can exist in a world that also holds so much pain. All the effort brought me here, to this place of spiritual depth. I know that I am exactly where I need to be. I am part of something so much bigger than myself. I am a thread in the spiritual fabric of our world, connected to everyone and everything. And when you can see that big picture...there is no better view.

One of my favorite Bible verses is Ecclesiastes 3:1-8: "For everything there is a season, and a time for every matter under Heaven: a time to be born, and a time to die; a time to plant, and a time to pluck up what is planted; a time to kill and a time to heal; a time to break down, and a time to build up; a time to weep and a time to laugh; a time to mourn, and a time to dance; a time to throw away stones, and a time to gather stones together; a time to embrace, and a time to refrain from embracing; a time to seek, and a time to lose; a time to keep, and a time to throw away; a time to tear, and a time to sew; a time to keep silent, and a time to speak; a time to love, and a time to hate; a time for war, and a time for peace."

I cry every time I read or hear this as it holds so much truth. I needed time to grieve. Time to process. Time to sit with my pain. I needed time to heal. Give yourself that time. Don't rush the journey, feel the pain of the loss. This phase does not last forever—it is a season. Allow it to be.

Joy also has its own season. And for me, it is now. It is my time to bask in the afterglow.

This healing journey has deepened my spirituality in ways I never could have expected. At the top of each of these mountains, I saw a glimpse of that vista view I was searching for—that wide, open panorama of the miraculous side of life. And now I find myself in the post-hike afterglow, reflecting on all the highs and lows of the journey, all the effort I put in to arrive here, and the deep connections I made along the way.

The deepest of those connections? My bond with Jack himself. One thing I now know for sure is that Jack is right here. In some ways he is with me more now because I think about him all the time—much more than I did before he passed over. From the first moments I met him after his birth to that last kiss on his cheek, the physical Jack was such a big part of my life. But now I see him in everything I do. I feel him in his favorite cup in the cupboard, in his picture on my dresser, smiling in his college sweatshirt with his arm around me. I feel him when I see a monarch butterfly, or a beautiful green and shiny dragonfly, or a bit of blue sea glass or white feather at the beach. Most of all, I see him in every person I meet who is openhearted, generous, joyful, and full of life.

Jack is still here, and we are closer than ever.

In some ways, Jack taught me to see. Learning to see him in the world after his body left us opened my soul to the possibility of a spiritual and miraculous world. I now see God in everything, much like I see Jack. In my awareness of Jack, I am also in alignment with my awareness of God all around me. God is leading me and protecting me in every aspect of my life. I see this perspective as a gift from Jack, directly from Heaven.

This awareness came in little incidents along my journey as blessings came into my life. In the initial shock of losing Jack, confronted with the devastating reality that he was gone, I was numb. I know now God had his arms around me in a shield of protection that manifested in a numbness to the pain. He kept me safe until I was ready to face reality.

God also used my grief to open my eyes to the stress of living in a marriage that had become dysfunctional. Keeping up my marriage was occupying my full concentration and zapping every bit of my energy. The stress level was toxic and I had arrived at a breaking point. Having my eyes opened was a gift that may not have happened if not for Jack's leaving. Having that stress gone has given me the energy to function and let in God's presence. It has given me space to find myself.

I also attribute to God all of the healing therapies that came to me soon after Jack died. There were too many coincidences, too many suspiciously timed referrals, too many perfect moments—where what I was learning in one modality built on another—for me to ignore God's hand in all of this. It all worked together to heal me enough, not only from the grief of losing Jack in such a traumatic way, but also from all the scars from my past.

God also knew that I would need the ocean to heal. I thought we had moved to Huntington Beach for Jack, so that he could train with the best water polo resources we could provide. It turns out, we also moved for me, I just didn't know it. That's exactly where I needed to be after Jack's death. I walked that beach every day for a year, and the ocean taught me, healed me, and molded me. It gave me a place to scream and cry and rage amidst the crashing waves. And it gave me so much opportunity to see Jack around me in the seashells, sea glass, and feathers he left on the sand.

And the people! God has used my pilgrimage to cross my path with so many incredible people. I swear, it's like all of our journeys were charted on a map just so we would walk alongside each other at exactly the right time. The yoga group I joined in an effort to heal brought me some of my best friends. I made new connections and deepened old ones on hikes and camping trips. I met my life coach, Lisa J., at just the right moment. How could that not be a gift directly from God above?

My life is full of friends who are here for me. I am never without some fun plan to meet up with one of them; in fact, my calendar is so full that I have to be careful to keep time for myself—a problem I see as a gift. It seems that just when I need a particular girlfriend's company, she appears in a text or phone call. I am so lucky to have so many wonderful friends—some dear friends for many years and some fairly new—come into my life in new ways to keep me from feeling too lonely. So many blessings on my path.

It is a glorious and chaotic web of confused cause and effect: In putting me on this path, Jack brought so many gifts into my life, including the capacity to see these gifts for what they are— God's plan for me. Each of these connections gave me a little more of what I needed to heal, but they also increased my belief in a connected and miraculous universe. And as that belief strengthened, more of these miracles happened in my life, and I became more able to recognize them. It's a beautiful tapestry of spiritual connection. I am now open to being surprised every day by how magical life can be.

One of the most surprising of those spiritual connections is, unbelievably, also a Jack. The first Mother's Day after Jack died was a tough one, but something miraculous happened that made it a little bit easier, a little God wink that filled my heart with love.

I attended Mother's Day service at my church, as was our family tradition. During the church service, I noticed a young man sitting in the front pew. I didn't remember ever seeing him before. I found myself staring at the back of his head; he looked just like my Jack! I could tell he was tall even though he was sitting down, and he had the mop of blonde hair, broad shoulders, and even a red polo shirt just like one of Jack's favorite shirts. It was uncanny. Here I was, tears rolling down my face because a stranger looked like my precious son whom I missed, especially on that morning.

After the service, my mom and I joined the line of parishioners waiting to greet Reverend Cindy, as is the custom at our church. While we were waiting, several people left the line and headed to get a mimosa. (I know, awesome church, right?) Suddenly, I found myself standing directly behind the young man I couldn't keep my eyes off throughout the church service! I put on my sunglasses to hide the tears filling my eyes as I watched him hug Cindy with what looked to be his grandmother by his side. They exchanged a few words before he and his companion moved on. I could hardly contain my emotions.

As I stepped up for my greeting, and Cindy realized it was me, her eyes widened. She glanced toward the retreating back of the young man.

"Julie, that young man I was just talking to..." she started.

"I couldn't help but notice him," I said. "He reminded me so much of Jack."

"I know!" she exclaimed and proceeded to tell me about this young man. He had just moved to the area from Northern

California to attend a local college on a water polo scholarship. Other than his grandmother, he had no family in the area.

Then, with a big smile, she added, "You're not going to believe this…his name is Jack!"

I was dumbfounded. The similarities to my Jack took my breath away. He even had the same brown birthmark on his right elbow! I mean, really! And then, just like a ghost, he was gone. I felt like I got to see my son on Mother's Day. I was so grateful for this little glimpse of Jack on such a difficult day. He had attended church only for this holiday, so I doubted I would see him again, but that glimpse was enough.

Then, over two years later, I got a call from Reverend Cindy. She said that the young man named Jack, the water polo player who had attended service two Mother's Days ago, had returned to our church the previous Sunday. She told Jack and his grandmother about me and my Jack, how similar they are, how I had lost Jack three years ago, and I felt my seeing him on Mother's Day two years ago was a gift.

It turned out that Jack did not have a strong support system. The lady with him was not his biological grandmother, but someone who had essentially adopted him as a surrogate grandson and was a big advocate for him.

Before she ended the call, Cindy added, "I'll send you a photo of a note Jack wrote."

A minute later I received a picture of a piece of paper with the words "I would love to meet you. Let's get lunch soon—Jack."

I told Cindy that I needed a few days to absorb this. I started having fear of what other people would think. Would it seem weird for me to want to meet this young man? Then I decided I really didn't care what other people thought. I wanted to meet him, so I sent a text that very day. We decided to have lunch after Sunday service.

That Sunday happened to be St. Francis of Assisi Day, a day the church has a Blessing of the Animals, including a pet parade. Like I said, awesome church! I had my rambunctious little tank of a dog, Lacey the Frenchie, with me, dressed in her Halloween pajamas. Jack and I had agreed to meet at a restaurant right after service. I saw the tall silhouette approaching and, quieting my sudden nerves, I waved him over. With a big smile he approached and I couldn't help but jump up and hug him. It felt like the natural thing to do and he reciprocated.

I'm not sure whether Jack was also a little nervous, but he seemed at ease as he began sharing about his school and sports activities. I didn't ask any questions about his family, but he openly shared anyway. He said his family was unconventional: His father was in a wheelchair from a spinal cord injury and not able to be there for him, and his mother was often busy caring for his sister who suffered from schizophrenia. His friends were his family here in Southern California.

I can't believe how this came together: a mom who had lost her son and a son without present parents. Lacey was not behaving (not a surprise, the little troublemaker), so I had to leave soon after we finished our meal. The goodbye was quicker than I wanted. But he invited me to attend a water polo game, and I told him I would. One more hug and I was out the door.

The hug felt so familiar, almost like a hug from both Jacks. I remember once seeing an interview with a father who, when he met the transplant recipient of his daughter's heart, he used a stethoscope to listen to the beating heart. Here was this living person who was not his daughter, yet it was his daughter's heart bringing life to this woman. I felt this way when I hugged this young man, like I got to feel a little of my Jack's embrace, and that meant the world to me.

Of course, I *do* realize this Jack is not my son. But I hope to be there for him as a support, another member of his pseudo family. We share a mutual respect for mother-and-son relationships and how special they are. I lost the tangible aspect of mine with my Jack, but maybe I could offer that love in support of this young man by being another caring person in his life.

I did attend several of Jack's water polo games after our meeting. The first time felt so surreal, walking up to the pool deck amidst the familiar sounds of the water splashing, the whistle blowing, the announcer broadcasting, the crowd cheering. I walked through the gate just as Jack made a goal, and the announcer bellowed, "Jack G. scores!" OMG, it was such strong déjà vu I felt like I was dreaming. I sat on the bleachers, feeling nervous and completely out of place, like I was a fraud to be there. I waved at Jack so he knew I was there, the only one to cheer him on.

A mother from the opposing team asked who my son was on the team, and I explained that I was a friend not a mother. She told me about her kids and kept asking questions about mine. I did eventually tell her that my son had been a water polo player for UCI. I told her he was deceased, and this was my first water polo game since he died three years before. She gave me a little side hug and a look of sincere compassion. I think she was an angel sent to help me through that first game, not as a parent of one of the players but as a friend.

Watching that game felt so different. Spectating cannot match the intense invested emotion of watching your own kid compete in a sport they love. I remembered the pride I felt watching my Jack make a goal as the center. He was so tough, so skilled. I thought about it later that night as I went to bed, why this game felt so different for me. It was like being given my favorite food, prepared and presented beautifully, and biting into it to find it had no taste at all. I loved water polo because *Jack* was playing. Without him, watching the match did not produce the same intensity in me.

I asked myself, "Why are you doing this to yourself?"

Yet I was so happy to be there for this Jack, to show my support of him. This game was about him, not me. The mom next to me made me feel less alone. When the game was over, Jack came by and chatted for a few minutes, thanking me for being there and telling me how much that meant to him. For me, that was reason enough to keep showing up. I am not questioning it too much, just seeing where our friendship will go and happy to have the opportunity to be a surrogate parent on the side of the pool. We all need love in this world to survive, and it sometimes comes in unexpected and wonderful ways. I can offer that to this Jack.

The pull to parent is so strong after you lose a child. The warrior parent spirit we had nurtured needs somewhere to go. It is healing to find an outlet for that love. And this new Jack in my life needs it too! I really can't believe this unimaginable connection—a truly magical and miraculous event, something I am experiencing in so many areas in this new world I now inhabit.

You, too, can witness magic through your own healing and openness to experiences that may seem unbelievable. I encourage you to embrace every one of the opportunities that come your way without worrying what others may think. I am here for you as a support. I will hold your hand and cheer for you from the sidelines.

We are in this world together, we are all connected. Can you feel it?

Another cosmic experience was meeting Lorne Cramer, the artist who designed this book's cover. Lorne creates digital mosaics that combine thousands of small photos into the image of one larger photo. Most of his works are portraits, especially of loved ones who have died. I saw his work at my friend Kim's home. As I mentioned before, she commissioned three mosaics made up of thousands of pictures of Connor from throughout his life.

When I began writing this book, I envisioned a cover art that would truly resonate with the themes of healing and remembrance. I got Lorne's contact information from Kim and reached out to him, introducing myself and sharing how much I admired his work. Lorne explained that he creates his art to aid those who have lost loved ones in their healing journey. He sees photos as the only visual proof that someone once existed, and he believes a mosaic can encapsulate the essence of a person through countless memories. The concept of "A Thousand Little Memories" really spoke to me. I ended up having an hour-long conversation with Lorne during that first call. He agreed to design my book cover and, naturally, wanted to hear all about Jack.

Then he shared wisdom I had never heard before, the truths related to quantum physics that I shared in Chapter Eleven. I was new to this information, and he has an understanding of the quantum universe better than anyone I've ever met. He was the person who first told me that conservation of energy could give a scientific explanation for the fact that Jack was so clearly still with me. Our talks became the basis for my theory that the mom warrior energy I had developed for Jack still exists. He connected my spiritual beliefs and experience to scientific theory in ways that blew my mind. It never occurred to me that the energy of each of us is part of the physical world, not somewhere out there in another dimension—kind of like I had always pictured Heaven's pearly gates. This really changed my understanding of what happens after we pass over.

Lorne and I have had several more thought-provoking conversations about apparent coincidence that seem to be connected somehow. He feels these happenings are not coincidence, but quantum entanglement. Two particles can link together in such a way that no matter how far apart they are in space, a change induced in one will affect the other. This was described by Albert Einstein as "spooky action at a distance." Lorne believes this theory accounts for happenings that seem random but fit into a pattern. They are actually connected in the quantum field.

Then I met Carol, who is also writing a book with my publisher, Hope Publishing House. Her story about a near-death experience and the profound lessons it taught her deeply inspired me. I wholeheartedly believe her account. The beautiful experience she had at age twelve has brought me peace about Jack's journey. She was shown a reality where everything is interconnected, and judgment and control are unnecessary. Her experiences resonate with what I've come to understand. We truly are all in this together, and there are no coincidences.

Whenever I meet someone who has lost a child, I don't have to say a word. There is a cosmic connection. We have an unsaid knowing and an immediate bond. I interviewed three women for this book who have lost a son, and I have that bond with all three. I scheduled each interview as I needed them for my writing schedule, and remarkably, unbeknownst to me, all three interviews were within a week of the anniversary of their son's death. They were already thinking of their child and reliving their grief when they received my call. All three young men died in the month of October. This seems random, but is it? Perhaps we are all quantumly entangled, connected no matter how far apart.

Are you also noticing coincidences or magical connections in your life? Perhaps they are more significant than we realize. Staying open to the possibility that these connections are meaningful can be comforting. It suggests that our experiences might not be random but could be intricately woven together. Many people go about their daily lives without pausing to consider the miracles of life, the earth, or the universe. I choose to seek out these miracles. Experiencing a profound loss, like the death of a child, often brings thoughts of our own mortality and a deeper appreciation for life. Such losses can draw us closer to a sense of the divine.

I find God in the cosmic connections that seem to appear more frequently now. The bond I share with my cousin Laura, as we support each other through our shared loss of a son, is a testament to this. Meeting my neighbor Kim shortly after Jack's death, who has shown me how to navigate grief with both sorrow and laughter, is another example. There's also Betsy, who lost her son Jack and has become my mentor in grief recovery, inspiring me to hike the Camino and live a fulfilling life after loss. The links between my Rick Steves trip to Italy with Jack, my seashell collection, and the symbolism of seashells in St. James Church in Newport Beach and the Camino de Santiago all weave together beautifully. I also cherish the connection with the young water polo player named Jack at church, Lorne's art that perfectly matched my needs, and Carol's story, which brought me peace about Jack's journey to the other side.

How can this all be just pure coincidence?

I believe it is divine guidance. My awareness of God in my life is putting me in a flow with the universe and the power of the Holy Spirit. I find that the more I focus on God and trust the universe, and not worry about how things will work out, the more peace and joy I can experience.

I watched a movie recently, *I Can Only Imagine*, the story behind the hit song by MercyMe. The movie is based on the true story of the lead singer, Bart Millard, and his dysfunctional childhood. Millard's father was extremely abusive toward him and his family, but he became a different person after a cancer diagnosis led him to find Jesus. The relationship between father and son eventually healed. After his father died, Millard wrote the song about his father in Heaven, and how he can only imagine what it must be like to meet Jesus.

As I did my daily run the morning after seeing the movie, I found myself singing the lyrics out loud. When I got to the line "I can only imagine, what it will be like to walk by Your side, surrounded by Your glory," tears sprang to my eyes. I don't have to imagine. I feel that I know what it is like to walk in God's presence, surrounded by the nurturing power of the universe. I made it to the top of the Mountain, and the view from the summit showed me a world of miracles. God is with me always, entangling me with all of creation. And so is Jack. I don't have to imagine Heaven. My perfect, kind-hearted, larger-than-life Jack has shown me that it's right here, waiting for all of us on our pilgrimage to joy.

So join us! Jack and I will see you there, basking in the beauty of life.

I Am That Mom

I am that mom, the one who lost a child to suicide.

But I am also that mom who was able to take the rough trail up the mountains of grief to the limitless world at the summit.

I am that mom who was able to heal her broken heart and find joy in life once more.

I am that mom who has given up on expectation by learning to live in the moment, embracing the quantum world—where Jack's energy flows—that is found in the possibility of the unknown. Connecting to the present moment puts me in alignment with the spiritual world and allows the amazing miracle of life to lead me on a path I never thought was possible.

I am that mom who guides others through the mountains of grief. I realize that the joy I can bring to others is greater than the loss I experienced, and, in fact, it is because of this loss that I have moved forward to helping others. My story has energy and is now a part of the quantum field. In sharing my experience, I create this energy for each of you reading these words.

I am that mom who is becoming more and more of the woman she is destined to be each day.

I am also a human who still stumbles along my path. I have days when I question the direction I have taken.

I finished the first draft of this book with a sense of euphoria, flying on the high of imagining all the people who would read my story and find their own way up the mountains of grief. I joined my coach, Lisa J., for an author's retreat in Maui, where all the authors in our program would come together to discuss the next steps for us and our books. The first evening, the sunset sky erupted in breathtaking, spectacular golden hues in bright contrast against the azure blue ocean, the warm breeze ruffling our hair as we posed for some fun, marketing pictures, jumping in the air and laughing. I was moved by the joyful ukulele music and did a little impromptu hula. We filmed me dancing, and I described the joy and excitement of being near completion of my book. I was truly feeling light and free at that moment.

When I returned home and saw this video on Lisa's Facebook page, I started judging myself. I felt guilty! How can I talk so lightheartedly about losing my son? Did I look "too" happy? What would other people think? Shouldn't I be more sad or at least less jubilant? Ugh! I wanted to call Lisa and ask her to take down the video!

To add another layer of complexity, Maui had been devastated by deadly fires just five months before. The retreat had been planned before the fires, and Lisa had confirmed that tourists were still welcome before we arrived. I had even called several local businesses myself to get a feel for how tourists visiting might affect them. Each person said they were still healing from the trauma, but they were hopeful and needed tourists to visit for the area to recover. Still, I felt guilty as I watched my image dance without a care in the world, just a few miles north of the ashes of Lahaina.

But instead of giving in to the guilt, I went within. I did some tough soul searching. Why was I judging myself so hard for being happy? Why was I so afraid of being judged as uncaring or frivolous? Was I forgetting Jack and moving on?

I remembered one of the lessons of my pilgrimage: I can hold both. I can hold grief for the loss of Jack's physical presence *and* celebrate the life his spirit has led me to. I can feel deep sympathy and a desire to help the community of Lahaina *and* let the beauty of Maui inspire me. That's the astonishing resiliency I witnessed in the people there: the willingness to hold both heartbreak and hope. I felt a connection to this dichotomy in my own loss journey. Happiness does not negate the love for what we've lost, and joy is not frivolous. It is Life!

In doing the soul search, I realized I am living what I want to teach others, that there is joy to be had and to not feel guilty about it. I am capable of feeling authentic joy in the moment, but then judge it. I also am capable of releasing the shame of past trauma by speaking my truth yet also judge myself for exposing these things. This is how I have lived for so long: hiding from what I perceive as judgment from others which is exactly what has kept me in a place where I wasn't living fully. I want to be free!

What came to mind was a quote I remembered: "The truth shall set you free." But I didn't know the source. I looked it up and found the actual quote: "And ye shall know the truth and the truth shall make you free" (John 8:32 KJV). It was a quote from Jesus! Wow! This was all I needed to be brave, to let go of the generational shame that had held me back and to speak my truth. I want to be free from hiding behind walls of shame that have dictated my life. I want to feel the authentic joy of living without guilt or judgment.

In doing this soul search I also realized that by experiencing joy again, I am not forgetting Jack, I am allowing him to shine through me. His joy is now my joy, and by releasing this joy and embracing it is to embrace Jack. Looking at the photos of me and the other authors jumping in the air on the beach gives me a happy feeling; we are living our best life in a magnificent place that is moving forward from its big loss. Bad things happen in life—this is a truth and a guarantee. Some people experience bigger losses than others, but every loss is big to the one experiencing it. The goal in life is to find a way through the effects of the loss, to grieve and heal and to experience it but to also realize there is hope on the other side of the loss. Take the lesson from your loss and help others with their journey. We are all one in our humanity. Our stories are intertwined to create a beautiful tapestry of life. Without the dark colors, the vibrant ones would not stand out. Living life without judgment is to experience joy.

I am that mom who has uncovered the truth of joy. I am a healer of pain. I stand for Jack, my son, and all the lessons he has taught me in both life and death.

Tori's Letter

My brother was one of the most popular kids in my entire school. He was a champion, a hero, a lover—absolutely adored by everyone. I think the hardest part about the rapid decline of his mental health was the fact that nobody expected it. We didn't know how to handle such a foreign situation.

Prior to the quarantine, Jack was one of the only people I understood to be legitimately happy with his life. So many kids around me were depressed, and he was a diamond in the rough: always there to uplift everyone, to inspire them with his reckless enthusiasm and his charm. But when he was the one who was struggling, many people made a mockery of him. No one understood that he was schizophrenic—somehow they thought he had spontaneously morphed into a terrible person. People pushed him away instead of embracing him—even me. I was confused and heartbroken by his behavior. I didn't know how to talk to him when it was so hard to get past the uncommunicative barrier of his psychotic behavior.

What I came to learn is this: The most important thing to remember about people in severe psychological crises is that the best you can do—and what you should do, if you can—is be present in their lives. Even if that feels pointless, even if you think you can't help that person, even if you can't get through to them, they still need you in their life. Their illness might transform them into a person you no longer recognize, but they aren't dead until they take that last breath.

Because of how common mental illness has become, the prospect of being inspired or carried through our lives by people like Jack has faded into a naive illusion. Even people like Jack have a breaking point. None of us are saviors, but we are companions. That's all we need to be. Bereavement is the deepest, darkest, most sporadic yet permanent emotion the average human can experience. And when you grieve a person who has died by suicide, bereavement becomes comorbid with another damaging emotion: regret. The most I can say is this: Don't be afraid to go above and beyond. Don't leave any room for regret. Be a companion to your loved ones, and remind them how much they mean to you every day.

NOTES